Alaska, No Regrets

Ray Savela

2009

Sales of this book benefit the White Bear Unitarian Universalist Church, Mahtomedi, Minnesota.

This book is a memoir, a reflection of the author's memories decades after related events took place.

For reprint permission, contact the author via Charlotte Preston: getsitdone@aol.com.

Printed and bound in Canada
www.ArtBookbindery.com

ISBN 978-0-615-30922-4

This book is dedicated

to my wife, Lucy (1927 – 1986)

and to our children

Jerry, Judy, Jewel, John, and June

whose Eskimo names are

Deegigalook, Givuduk, Buningjung, Lapsin, and Ahkowak

And, Patti dear, thanks for sharing a great sense of humor

which is our way to express our love for one another

and the glue and adhesiveness that keeps us hitched.

Thanks

to my friends Charlotte Preston and Mary Kurth

for listening, inputting, editing, and helping me publish my story.

Thanks to Cheryl Weiberg for editorial work on earlier publications.

CONTENTS

PREFACE

I love to write and tell stories, and I may not be around long to continue this great pleasure of mine, because I am over 80 years old.

My mother used to call me Number One. I thought I was the best, but over the years I discovered Number One was the worst. What I learned from experience was to grade myself starting with Number One as worst and the higher numbers as better.

When I was about 7, my mother bought me a nice second-hand coat with no buttons on it. My mother sewed on some large buttons and sent me outside to see if the coat was warm. I loved it. But for some reason, I started twisting the buttons one by one till they all came off.

When I went back in the house, my mother asked me, "Where are the buttons?"

"In my pocket. I twisted them off."

She started to laugh. My mother did have a sense of humor at times. It was about this time, though, that she said, "Irvin, if you don't behave yourself, you will never get our inheritance." This story illustrates that I've been graded upside down all my life. If I give myself a grade for twisting off the buttons, it would be a 7. Why do I do so many dumb things? It's because I got started on the wrong end of the numbers.

My mother did have her way. She disowned me because I married an Eskimo girl.

Item XII

"Disinheritance Specific. I intentionally and with full knowledge of the consequences do not provide in this will for my son, Ray Savela. I intend that this disinheritance specifically defeat the application of any statutory heirship interest including, but not limited to, a claim for exempt property allowance, family allowance and a homestead exemption."

Ma! I want to say this to you because you are my mother. I don't understand why I was disowned. Being rejected I don't understand. I certainly wasn't perfect, but I don't believe I was bad either. Marrying Lucy was the smartest thing I ever did in my life. My only family residing in Alaska now are with Eskimo blood. I am proud of it.

Even though I know you can't hear me, I have a few things to say. I never hated you. I remember the hard times and the good times. I forgive you deeply in my heart. I said "I love you," the day before you died. I know some of the Finns are dour – but not all of them. You and Pa had a good sense of humor, but it wasn't our nature to say, "I love you," or give each other a big hug. I did learn to kiss and hug Lucy, and we did it all the time. It's been more than twenty years since Lucy died. Me and Pat, who you called "the other woman," express our feelings all the time, too.

It's time for me to forgive and forget and cast the albatross from my neck and say, "I love you, Ma." I am writing this paper to let you know I forgive you, Ma, and also to release me from that bondage while my mind is still clear. Ma, I feel like a free man now.

(signed) Raynold I. Savela

BORN TO FINNS

1925 Born to Finns

I was born Raynold Irvin Savela in Minneapolis, Minnesota, in General Hospital. My parents, Hilda Maria Siironen and John Savela, both born in 1904, married in 1921. Bruce was born in 1922. My parents, who called me "Irvin" were just 21 when I was born March 6, 1925. They spoke Finnish to each other at home and English to us. We learned Finnish names of animals and daily things, but I learned to speak English before I started school.

My parents bought a farm near Braham, Minnesota, not far from Cambridge. This little farm was not large enough to support a family, so my dad got a job selling Ford automobiles in Cambridge. Our farmhouse set up on a little hill. On either side were the blueberry bogs. My mother's mother gave my parents a team of horses. We also had a pig and chickens. When we first moved there, we bought milk from a neighbor. Bruce said, "Mama, do you know where that milk is coming from?" When we got our own cow we understood it better.

Our house wasn't very big, but I thought it was really nice. There was a parlor and a large open front porch. The main floor had one bedroom where my parents slept and a fair-sized kitchen that had a steep, narrow staircase from the unfinished room upstairs. The upstairs was not plastered, just lathe on the wall, dry as kindling. Uncle Willard (age 8), Bruce (6), and I (4) all slept upstairs in the same bed.

Uncle Walter's Joke

My mother's brother came from Menahga to visit us. Walter was a young man, about 20 years old, and was sporting a mustache. Bruce thought our uncle looked so neat! He wanted a mustache too. He asked Uncle Walter how he could get one.

"That's easy! Just follow that big rooster. When he lets a big poop come out, take some of that goo-goo and smear it under your nose."

When we sat down for supper, my Ma said, "What do I smell? Someone must have stepped in some chicken doo doo."

Uncle Walter didn't say a thing. We all checked our shoes. Everyone said, "Mine are OK."

Ma wasn't convinced. She got close to Bruce. "What's that under your nose?"

"Uncle Walter told me to put it there so I could grow a mustache like he has."

Ma took Bruce outside with a wash basin to scrub his face, and she scolded her brother for doing such a nasty trick.

1928 Lightning Storm

One evening, as he usually did for laundry day, my Pa filled the wash tub in the kitchen from the water pump outside between the house and the barn. He prepared additional pails of water so my Ma could wash clothes the next day.

During the night there was thunder and lightning, and it rained hard. Lightning struck the house, close to our bed, and ignited the wall in a second. The sound was like an explosion. The three of us boys jumped out of bed and headed down the stairs as fast as we could go.

My mother climbed up the stairs with a bucket of water and told Willard and Bruce to keep bringing her water so she could throw it on the burning wall. Our mother, Bruce, and Uncle Willard put the fire out. I was too young to help. I just cried and tried to stay out of everybody's way. It was by the gift of God that my mother was going to wash clothes the next day and Pa had the water ready in the kitchen.

Where was my Pa while all this was going on? When the lightning struck the house, a big portion of the plaster fell on him and knocked him out. The falling plaster also killed our little dog in the kitchen porch. I don't know if they could have carried my Pa out of the bedroom if Ma, Willard, and Bruce hadn't put the fire out.

I don't know how long it took my Ma to bring my dad conscious. It took about a year before his memory functioned normally. During that time, Pa had to write down where he was going or what he intended to do.

Shortly after the fire Ma became very sick. She had to go to the hospital. I'm not sure if my dad was able to drive yet. I don't know if my dad went with my mother, or if anyone was staying with us boys. This may have been the one-time emergency I remember when my mother drove a car by herself. I was in my mid-50s before my mother finally told Bruce and me that we would have had a sister, but that she'd had a miscarriage right after the fire.

Saw-Rig

A neighbor came over to our house with his saw-rig to cut wood for winter. Sawing wood occupied both men's attention so they didn't notice what this little boy was up to, playing with my ball. My Pa and his helper must have stepped away from the saw-rig to get another log. They didn't see me, but from the porch my Ma did. She saw me crawling towards the saw-rig to reach for my ball. It had settled in the saw-dust groove directly under the saw blade. Ma got my dad's attention without screaming. My dad sneaked up behind me, pushed my face into the saw dust and pulled me by my leg so that I was safely clear of the saw blade. Then he spanked me, and I didn't know why. But I knew to stay away from the saw-rig.

Full of Smoke

One day my Ma went down the hill to the bog to pick blueberries. I followed her to eat some berries, too. With my short legs, I had trouble climbing over the bushes. I knocked berries to the ground. I was just a big nuisance.

Ma said, "Irvin, go back to the house so I'll have time to pick berries."

I waddled back to the house and opened the door. The house was full of smoke. I waddled back to tell Ma. Before I got all the way back, Ma yelled at me, "Go back!"

"I can't go in. It's full of smoke." Ma dropped her berry basket and raced up the hill to the house. Yes, the house WAS full of smoke.

Our neighbor Mr. Lind was working on our field. Ma ran toward him and yelled that the house was full of smoke. Mr. Lind ran to the house. He peered in the door to see if he could locate where the fire was. It seemed close to the kitchen stove. He crawled on his hands and knees towards the stove and doused the small fire. The stove door must have been held open a little by a longer piece of wood when the wood was shoved into the stove. Hot coals had dropped out and burnt a hole right through the floor.

1929 Country School

I was an active kid wandering around where I shouldn't be, so my mother decided to send me two miles down the road to the country school. I was 4. Uncle Willard was 8 and my brother Bruce was 6. Of course they got to school way ahead of me. I sat in the corner most of the time, thinking this was a privileged place for the smart kids. The enrollment was twenty kids. The teacher married one of the eighth graders. Maybe she had to marry him to help him pass the eighth grade.

1930 Foreclosure

My folks were unable to make their payments for the farm mortgage. They owed $800. The bank foreclosed on the farm. The bank must have taken everything except a one-cylinder engine that my dad managed to bring to my grandpa's farm so he didn't have to pump water for 30 cows by hand. The bank must have felt generous, because they let my dad keep his car. I always wondered what happened to the horses and the cow, pig and chickens and our big wooly outdoor dog Bear. I suppose they were all sold at auction.

All we had was our clothes. We didn't have a pickup or trailer to haul anything anyway. We stayed with an elderly couple for two or three days before we drove to Duluth.

1930 Duluth

Duluth was an exciting city. There wasn't any development on the high hills. It was fabulous. Bruce and I liked to go up on the Aerial Bridge when the guard was on the other side. The interesting city dump was right where the city sport arena is in 2009.

We walked to where the big slide was that went into the lake. It was about five miles from where we lived just off of Superior Street, with its gentle hill where the street car went. I think you needed money to use the slide, so we never tried it. We couldn't swim anyway.

We played on the Bay side because the water of Lake Superior was warmer there. Bruce didn't always want me to go with him, because he was trying to smoke cigarette butts he picked up wherever he found them. I never did tell our Ma. I guess we were little bums. I couldn't go to school because the Duluth authorities said I was too young.

1932 Half Team Dog Race

When I was about seven years old there was an article in the <u>Minneapolis Tribune</u> that an Alaska dog team would visit the city and demonstrate how dogs are used in Alaska. There were maybe six or eight in the team. I have a strong feeling this team belonged to Leonard Seppala or Mrs. Seppala because her dogs were all white. (He was the man that carried the last leg of the race to deliver the valuable diphtheria serum to Nome from Nenana.) After the Alaska dog team finished their demonstration, the professional dog musher gave assistance to organize the Half Dog Team race. I'm calling it a Half Dog Team race because it requires two dogs to make a team, but all of us amateurs had only one dog. It wasn't any easy task to organize about 25 or 30 dogs and the same number of kids. This race wasn't anything like the Iditarod or the Fairbank's North American Championship race. The big time dog races allowed one team to leave the chute every two or three minutes, no confusion. The Minneapolis race had all 25 or 30 dogs lined up side by side. What a mess! All the dogs were barking, some were fighting, and we kids were trying to hold our dogs back and yelling at them till we got the "go" signal.

My little Nikki was a feisty little fart. He wanted to chase the other big dogs right away. Nikki took off like a rocket, yipping and yapping all he could. But suddenly he hunched up and started to poop. He must have been a little constipated because he had trouble discharging a turd. I tried to urge him with the sled but he was just sliding along. People behind the fence were yelling, "Come on pup. Keep going." Nikki and me we came in last.

Everyone was hanging around the news reporter while the judges determined who the winners were. The reporter was writing names down and asking questions. His back was toward me so I couldn't get his attention.

"Back off Kid, can't you see I'm busy?"

"Yes, but I want to talk to you when you're through."

"OK! OK! Just wait a few minutes." I had a break. The newspaper man turned towards me.

"OK Kid. What's so special about your dog?"

I said, "I have the smallest dog."

"By George, you do have the smallest dog. When did you finish?"

I said, "We were the last ones in because my Nikki had to poop."

"Fair enough. I'll try to get it in the paper." And he did. The paper said the harness broke.

1932 Lead Nickel

My Ma called me to come into the house one day. She was dropping a coin on the table.

"Why are you doing that, Mom?"

"Because I don't think it's a real nickel."

"Let me see it, Ma. It looks OK to me. It has a buffalo and a date on it."

"That's right, but it doesn't sound like a real nickel."

"Ma, can I have it?"

"No! You can't have it because you might try to spend it."

"No, Mom, I won't try to spend it. Honest, Ma. Please! Cross my heart and hope to die if I'm telling you a lie."

My mom finally broke down and gave me the nickel and I put it in my pocket and said, "Thanks, Ma." When I went outside, I felt rich, and I kept wondering if Ma was really right about the nickel. Now I had a feeling that the Devil was prying into my brain trying to coax me to spend the nickel. *No! I won't do it. I promised my Mom.*

My best friend Eddie that lived upstairs of our house was coming down the outdoor steps, and said, "Hi! Irvy. Whatcha doing?"

"Nothin'."

"Whatcha got in your pocket? A frog or something that's going to jump out?"

"Aww, it's just an old nickel. I don't want to lose it."

Eddie said, "Can I see it?"

"Aww, I guess. My Ma said it wasn't real."

"Sure it is. Let me feel it. . . Hey! This is real. I know how we can tell."

"My Ma said, 'Don't try to spend it.'"

Eddie said, "Listen to this. I've got a master plan. We go to a store and spend it on candy. If we get the candy, it means it's OK. If they don't sell us the candy, it means there is something wrong with it and we just walk out. How does that sound?"

I felt kind of queasy about Eddie's master plan, but I said OK anyway. We went to a store my mother never shopped in and stood in front of the candy display case till the store keeper came over and asked us, "What can I do for you boys?"

I said, "We would like a nickel's worth of candy." I pointed to what we wanted. The store keeper put the candy in a bag and slid it over the counter. I laid my nickel down very carefully. I dashed out, ran across the street and squatted in the bushes in an empty lot. The store keeper plunked the coin on the counter before we were even out of the store. He was right behind us and grabbed our bag of candy. He didn't even give me my nickel back.

We went home discussing Eddie's master plan and our failed escape. Eddie and I played around the house for a while until Eddie went upstairs to his house and I went into ours.

Ma greeted me at the door and said, "I was just going to call you, Irvin. I'll need your help to carry groceries home."

"OK, Ma." Up the street we went. Ma headed toward the store where Eddie and I tried to spend the lead nickel.

"Ma! Why are you going to that store? You never shopped there before."

"I know it, Irvin, but they have something that's on sale that I need."

I didn't face the store clerk. I was trying to hide behind my mother, but it didn't work. The clerk looked at me and asked, "Is that your son?" And of course my mother had to say yes.

I just ran out the door and burst into tears and cried all the way home. My mother didn't scold me or spank me, but the crying and the screaming started all over again when Ma told my dad the story. My mom thought I was punished enough to live with my guilt.

(P.S. Listen to your momma.)

1932 Minneapolis

We must have lived in Duluth for about two years before my dad was given an offer for an increase in wages from Minneapolis Coca Cola. That's why we moved to north Minneapolis.

We lived in four different houses in North Minneapolis, two in South Minneapolis, wherever the rent was the cheapest. We moved many times. Bruce and I checked the garbage cans for saleable metal and bottles. We loved the dump! I cut my feet on broken bottles.

Something happened that we didn't understand then. Bruce and I were wakened in the night. Ma and Pa were fighting. Pa was trying to open the window, Ma was trying to close it. The room smelled of gas. Pa was bruised and scratched. Ma and Pa never knew we knew.

The fifth house was the best, but we had to leave because we couldn't afford it. My dad went to work for Clausen and Thill, a company that sold the best beer and soft drinks. Now he had customers in the city and in the country.

Bruce discovered there was a lake not too far away from our new place. Bruce and I still couldn't swim, but we enjoyed playing in the water. My mother and another lady sitting on a nearby bench started talking. She asked my mother if she had any kids.

"Yes, they're playing out there in the water."

"I don't see any white kids out there," the lady replied. Bruce and I spent so much time playing in the water we turned really black.

Times were hard. Bruce and I picked coal from the tracks. We found dry wood by the river – we piled it up. We helped Pa pull it up the steep bank. We explored the caves – they were scary.

A Trick on Uncle Johnny

Our house in Minneapolis was typical of the mid-1930s, with one bedroom, a kitchen, and a dining room with the coal stove. The dining room also served as a bedroom for my brother Bruce and me. This room joined the sitting room through a large archway. We all took our baths in a round washtub in the middle of the kitchen floor and we washed our faces and hands in a basin in the kitchen sink with water heated in a tea kettle. The kitchen was where all the action took place. All the work was done there and it also served as our dining area.

It was a special day. Uncle Johnny was coming to visit. And my mother was making donuts. Oh, My! Bruce and I could hardly wait to sink our teeth into them.

"It's no use drooling over the donuts, because you're not getting any till your Uncle Johnny gets here," Ma said. "You just as well go out and play till he arrives."

"OK, Ma. We won't be far away," Bruce and I chimed in.

"Before you go out, hold onto this chair for me while I take a look into the top cupboard."

"OK, Ma," I said. My mother was moving jars and bags around up there.

"Hurry up, Ma. I want to go out and play."

"Don't get in a hurry, now. You have all day to play." All of a sudden Ma let out a scream and said, "Oh, my Gosh! You won't believe what I found up here."

"What is it, Ma? What is it?" I shouted, thinking maybe she found a dead mouse.

"Do you remember the time I made donuts a couple of months ago?"

"Ja."

"Well, there's about a dozen donuts still here. I hid them from you boys so you wouldn't gobble them up. Here, take them and throw them in the garbage. They're as hard as rocks."

"Hey, Ma. They look just like the fresh ones. Man, they sure are hard."

"Hang onto this chair. You can throw them out when I get down."

"OK, Ma." While Ma was still searching, little light bulbs started flashing in my head. A devil with horns and a twitching tail conjured up a plan. The devil said, *You can't throw those donuts out. You should serve them to Uncle Johnny.* My subconscious replied, *What a clever trick. We'll do it!*

"Irvin, hang onto the chair now. Then you can chuck those donuts out."

"OK, Ma. But I don't want to throw the donuts out. They look just as good as the fresh ones."

"So what. You can't eat them. They're too hard."

"No! No! We won't eat them. We'll serve them to Uncle."

"That's a good idea," Bruce said. "Let's serve them to Uncle Johnny." It was one of the few things we agreed on.

"Oh, you crazy boys! OK. Go ahead. Have your fun."

Bruce and I went out to play until Ma hollered for us to come in and wash our hands. We set the table with coffee cups and spoons, the sugar bowl and cream pitcher and of course a plate full of donuts. The hard ones faced where Uncle Johnny would sit.

Ma said, "You had better clear off the table and then fill the plate after the coffee is made, or your Uncle Johnny will think you're up to something." Ma was getting right into the act, too.

We could hardly wait. Finally Uncle Johnny arrived.

"Hi, Uncle Johnny!" Bruce and I said with big smiles.

"Hi, boys. Hi, Hilda."

Ma said, "Hi, Johnny. You're looking well. How are things going?"

"Just fine. How's John?"

"He's OK. He's working Saturdays now. He won't be home till after seven."

I started to say, "Uncle Johnny, would …"

Bruce kicked my shoe and whispered, "Not yet."

After a little chit-chat about the latest news, Ma said, "I'll put on a pot of coffee."

"Good," Uncle Johnny said.

"I'll set the cups, Ma," I said.

"I'll get the cream and sugar," Bruce said.

Finally, Ma said "The coffee is ready. Come in the kitchen, Johnny. I just made some fresh donuts."

We all sat down at the kitchen table. It seemed like Uncle Johnny would never quit stirring his coffee and talking.

"Have a donut, Uncle Johnny." Bruce and I each took one and started eating, both of us saying, "M-m-m-m. Good donuts, Ma."

We were all staring at Uncle Johnny. He didn't try biting the donut yet. He was still talking. Then . . . we all held our breaths . . . he bit the donut. Nothing happened. He started talking again and he tried dunking it. It didn't fit in his cup. Uncle Johnny pretended everything was OK and continued talking. Then he tried breaking the donut so it would fit into his cup.

That's when we burst out laughing and so did Uncle Johnny. He knew now it was all a trick.

"Have a fresh donut, Johnny," Ma said, and turned the plate around.

1932 Going to Grandpa's and Grandma's for Christmas

Ma and Pa, my brother Bruce and me, and my dad's sister Julie were all going on a trip to Sebeka, about 200 miles northwest of the Twin Cities, to visit Grandpa and Grandma for Christmas. It was a warm morning for late December, but my folks didn't take chances in the winter. They packed a couple of blankets and warm clothes in the car.

About half way to Sebeka, it started snowing. My folks weren't too concerned till we were about 30 miles away. By then, my dad had to slow down because the visibility was getting worse. The wind was picking up and the temperature was dropping. We had already had to back up once in a while to be able to drive ahead faster through a drift.

Ma said, "You kids better keep those blankets around you. Pa doesn't trust that manifold heater to run it in case it rusted the exhaust system. It could leak into the car."

"OK, Ma. We're warm." When we got to Sebeka it was snowing hard. Pa stopped the car to have a discussion with Ma. Should we go on or see if we could stay some place? I don't think there was a hotel, and there weren't any motels in those days.

Pa said, "Ma, let's give it a try." So we did.

It wasn't long before we got stuck. Pa couldn't go backward or forward. Pa had to take his shovel out and clear tracks for ten or twelve feet at a time. Pa couldn't see fence posts anymore. They were hidden mostly because of the blowing snow and darkness. The telephone poles were visible. Pa kept shoveling. But his track was on the edge of the ditch and so the right wheel pulled him off the road.

Pa said, "That's it! I'm played out. I can't shovel anymore. I think the next farm is Tolpi's." Pa told us to stay in the car till he got back. The Tolpi's farm was perhaps 150 yards from where our car was ditched. Pa banged on the door. Nobody answered the knock. Pa kept banging.

Finally Mr. Tolpi came and said, "Come in, John." They had a large family. Many shoepacks, socks, and mittens were around the wood stove. Our family sat on their chairs the rest of the night till Pa could phone Grandpa to let him know what was going on. I imagine Grandpa had to do his chores before he could come with the horses and sleigh to pick us up. Us kids thought it was the greatest fun to ride in the sleigh covered with quilts.

This Christmas was a happy one except for the storm, but even that had its rewards. The next day Grandpa took us back to the Tolpi's to tow our car out of the ditch with Prince and Beauty. We had already thanked Grandma so Grandpa didn't have to make another trip with the horses. Then Pa heated the car with hot coals from the stove to get the car going.

We thanked the Tolpis and Grandpa for the great Christmas holiday. I still have wonderful memories that have stayed with me all these years.

WHY DO I HAVE TO WORK SO HARD?

1935 Lake Nokomis

We moved to South Minneapolis and discovered Lake Nokomis. Bruce learned how to swim first and had lots of fun. I had to stay within the safety ropes until I learned. I could dog paddle and swim underwater, so I thought I was ready to try to swim out to the diving dock that was in deep water. I got halfway there and I almost panicked looking back at the ropes. But I decided it was just as far either way, so I kept dog paddling and got to the diving dock. After that experience, I started experimenting with a conventional stroke.

On the Fourth of July, there was a huge celebration at Lake Nokomis including pitching horseshoes, foot races, sack races, catch the egg, three-legged race and also a suntan contest. Bruce said, "Irvin, you can win that easy!"

"If that kid over there is entering, I'm not going in."

"You're a lot blacker than he is! You can't see your back," Bruce said. I entered and won first prize, $2.50 worth of groceries. That was a great prize. Our weekly grocery bill was about $3.00 for essentials. Some butcher shops would give you a pound of lard free. Butter was expensive in those days at 40 cents a pound, and it wasn't legal to sell oleo in Minnesota.

1935 Grandpa's Farm

My Grandpa had homesteaded in Lake of the Woods County in 1911 when my dad was seven years old. The home-stead was about five miles south of Graceton, right next to the Great Swamp. The old county road maps described a large area between Upper Red Lake and south of Graceton as the Great Swamp. My dad had always awakened me if we were going fishing or hunting by saying, "Wake up, Irvin. It's daylight in the swamp."

(Keith "Kit" Bergh, my beloved companion Patricia Bergh's late husband, was born in Baudette, MN, in Lake of the Woods County and also used, "daylight in the swamp." It gives me a notion that "daylight in the swamp" originated in Lake of the Woods County.)

A few days after school let out for summer vacation in 1935, my dad asked me if I wanted to spend the summer on Grandpa's farm at Sebeka. I could hardly believe what I was hearing. Of course I said, "Yes!" and jumped for joy. My brother Bruce and I always had fun at the farm. Besides the fun, we had good things to eat, like flat bread, wild June berries, milk and cream and large cookies with our coffee. We usually traveled to Sebeka once or twice a year to visit relatives. That's what made it so special.

This visit was much the same except for quite a different reason. The weekend visit was over, so my folks and Bruce headed for the cities about noon on Sunday. I didn't quite understand why Bruce wasn't staying, but I didn't care. He liked to boss and tease me. It would be a lot more fun without him anyway.

My Uncle Johnny and Aunt Julie were already on the farm. Aunt Julie was 15 years old and Uncle Johnny was 13 or 14. They were both going to school in the city when Grandma died and Grandpa was trying to run the farm by himself, which proved to be too much.

Grandpa was losing weight and became sick. Without a cook he wasn't eating properly.

Johnny and Julie were raised on this farm so they knew what to do; I wondered what my job would be. I was 10. I got my first lesson Monday morning when Grandpa woke me up at 4 a.m. He gave me a little nudge on the shoulder and said, "noseps ulus Órvenii (Wake out, Irvin)." That is how my day started and Grandpa never had to call me twice.

Grandpa showed me how much to feed the chickens and how much grain to put in the pigs' feed barrel that was replenished with buttermilk from the creamery in Sebeka. When I became proficient with the chickens and pigs, it was time to learn how much grain and hay the cows and horses needed. This routine went on every day of the week. The cows had to be milked exactly twelve hours apart. Grandpa was really strict about that. While Grandpa and Johnny were doing the milking, Julia got breakfast ready before she separated the cream and washed the separator. After the chores were done, we all ate breakfast together.

Grandpa had all the fields plowed. Now the soil was ready for us to pick rocks that came to the surface with the frost and load them on the stone-boat and haul them to the edge of the field. Next was to drag the field with the spike-tooth drag. Now the land was ready for planting. I would go with Grandpa out to the fields to plant, even though all I could do was follow him and the horses and help him fill the planting drill with seeds. Johnny would clean the barn and replace fence posts or do a dozen other things that needed attention. Aunt Julie washed dishes, baked bread, cooked, and planned for lunch and supper.

One time I was helping Aunt Julie with the kitchen rugs, rag rugs that went from wall to wall in the kitchen. These rugs had to be hauled outside and washed by hand. I saw Grandpa coming in with the team. I asked, "Why is Grandpa coming in so early with the horses?"

Julie thought for a few seconds and then gave a hysterical scream. "Oh! My God! We forgot Grandpa's 3 o'clock coffee." Grandpa didn't say a word. He just put the team in the barn. We didn't know where he went until chore time.

Something else happened that day. I've never forgotten. I complained to Aunt Julie, "Why do I have to work so hard, carrying buckets of water … (and a list of other things)?" When I faced Julie, I could see how tired she looked – then she started to cry. I felt so bad, "Don't cry, Auntie. I won't say that again. Please don't cry." I never complained after that.

Now that I was becoming a farmer, Grandpa decided I should be milking, so he introduced me to a short-horn heifer that would be milking soon. This youngster had never been milked. Her teats were so short and underdeveloped I had a hard time getting any milk. She would try to step on my foot and swat her tail to strike me on the head with a gob of manure. My legs were not accustomed to holding the bucket while I sat on a one legged stool. When I did manage to get a few squirts, the milk missed the pail or went up my sleeve. It was a good experience for me to start with a young heifer. When I got to milk an older cow, it was a snap. I did so well Grandpa promoted me with two more cows to milk. Later in the summer when the crops were coming up, I still had a chance to go with Grandpa out to the field where we would have coffee and cookies or fresh bread and jelly together.

Grandpa started cultivating corn that was about 4" tall. He made a couple of rounds and then he explained to me how the cultivator worked. The tillers were on each side of the cultivator, hung so they were suspended and you could steer them with your feet. If the spade was too close to the plant, you gave it a push to miss the plant. Grandpa turned me loose with the team and everything went well. The only problem was my legs were too short. I pulled four plants out. Grandpa walked the round that I just finished and saw the four plants I dug up. So I didn't get to drive the team anymore until Fall to put up hay.

Grandpa's horses were named Prince and Beauty. Oh! what faithful animals they were. They did everything Grandpa needed them for. One of the hardest jobs was to raise a heavy sling load of hay up to the hayloft opening. Sometimes it was hard for the horses to pull evenly. Grandpa would talk to them in Finn and they would pull together. Grandpa's horses didn't speak English, so you would be out of luck if you didn't know the language. They would just stand there and look at you. When any of his horses became too old to work, he retired them so they had free board and room until they died.

We put up hay, oats, and barley, picked pickles, picked potato bugs, cultivated the garden, carried wood in, emptied the slop pail, carried in water, milked the cows, fed the animals and many other things. After a day's work, sometimes I would fall asleep at the supper table. There didn't seem to be much time for Grandpa to tell stories.

I still wonder why our name was changed from Savineimi to Savela.

Grandpa wasn't a man you would call a swearing man, but if there was a call for it, he could sling out a few gems. One time when the hoist lines started to twist halfway up to the hayloft opening, Grandpa had the horses hold the load where it was until he got it untwisted. Grandpa climbed up on the hay rack, then on top of the hay load to try to untwist the double line, when suddenly it started to untwist by itself with Grandpa's thumb in between the two lines. Oh, wow, I heard some lovely new words – "Saatana Perkele – Perkele – Perkele"

Oh! how nice those new words sounded, especially "Perkele." The rolling "r's" were beautiful "r, r, r, r, r" like a motor boat.

"Are you OK, Grandpa?"

"Saatana Perkele!"

I guess he was OK. He still had his thumb. Swearing in Finnish doesn't sound bad like English bad words.

One time I met a Finnish minister at Two Harbors and asked him what "Saatana Perkele" meant. He said, "I can't use those words in my sermon." I think he skirted my question. "Something about the devil," he said.

I didn't have time to play but I really had a chance to get acquainted with my Grandpa, Uncle Johnny, Aunt Julie, and of course Prince and Beauty. My folks sent word they would be up the coming weekend to bring me home. I could hardly wait to tell them all the things I learned – except for the bad words.

I wasn't anxious to leave. I would like to have stayed and gone to school there, because all the kids spoke Finnish except a German brother and sister. "Oh, well," I thought. "Maybe I can come back next year and go to school."

The second summer, 1936, the picture changed somewhat. My aunt and uncle were unable to work on the farm that summer so it was my mother, Bruce, and me. I already felt like a seasoned farmer because I could tell my older brother how to do some of the work projects.

1937 Country Again – Bloomington

All of my dad's customers knew my dad John was looking for a place to rent. One day, one of his customers – Jud Thomas - said, "John, I've got a nice little place in Bloomington for rent if you're interested."

Pa asked, "How much?"

Jud said, "Can you manage $15 a month?"

Pa said, "Yes, we can manage that."

The house was really kind of like a shack, but we were happy with it even though it was really small. It only had three rooms and the ceiling was only about 6 ½' high. The kitchen was too small to dine in, so we ate in the common room that was large enough if the double bed was folded up. Ma and Pa slept in a narrow porch that was converted into a bedroom.

The plus part of this place was the eighty apple trees with a great variety of fruit, a team of horses, a little barn, a garage with a dirt floor and a double door that wasn't very snug, a chicken coop and ten acres of land. The negative was that some things weren't very convenient. The water pump was inside the fence in the orchard, so it was easy to water the horses, but to carry water into the house we had to spread the barbed wire apart to get through the fence. The barn wouldn't hold more than four horses, but it was big enough for the team belonging to Jud Thomas.

There was an outhouse behind the little one car garage. Bruce and I found a barrel that was cut in half to put on top of the outhouse for our shower. In the winter, we all took a bath in the little kitchen. My mother took her bath in the little garage in the summer.

My curiosity got the best of me once and I tried peeking through the cracks in the garage door, but it was so dark in there I couldn't see a thing. I'd never seen a naked woman, though we Finns used a sauna. When we went to sauna, the boys went with the men when the sauna was the hottest. The women took the little boys and little girls with them. In North Minneapolis there was a public sauna. One side for men and the other side for women.

The first time I saw a naked woman was at the Minnesota State Fair, where I saw an "exotic dancer" at age twelve.

1937 Young Businessmen

Bruce and I thought we could make a lot of money if Jud Thomas would let us use the horses to plow and cultivate the extra seven acres and plant sweet corn, musk melons and tomatoes. Jud agreed, if we gave him half of the net income. Bruce and I would each receive one quarter of the net. It really sounds dumb now. Jud should have paid us for taking good care of his horses. Anyway, we had visions of getting rich.

The horses behaved very well for us, even though they hadn't been harnessed for a long time. I had learned how to drive a team when I was on my grandpa's farm. We plowed this land that hadn't seen a plowshare for years. The sod was full of quack grass and it was a lot of work just to get the land ready to plant. Every day after school we needed to plow or weed or work the land. We planted our corn, melons and tomatoes and they did really great.

When our dad saw how well we were doing with our project he said, "You boys will need some transportation to sell your produce." My dad knew an old-timer who was too old to crank his '23 Model T, so he was willing to sell it for $7. All it needed was five new tires for $1.85 each and a set of transmission bands and it was ready to go.

Not many people bought our sweet corn for 10 cents a dozen. After the early market was over, we couldn't get 15 cents a bushel for our melons. We walked up and down trying to sell the produce, but not many takers. After we added up our expenses, gas and tomato boxes, Bruce and I earned $14 a piece. Jud Thomas' share was $28. People now say, "That wasn't bad for those days." Yes. It was bad for a full season of work.

After that experience, we worked at the local farms. In the fall Bruce and I worked carrying sweet corn to the edge of the field so it could be loaded on a truck. On an average day two pickers picked 800 to 1000 dozen ears of corn, 10 doz. to the stack. The most that was picked that fall was 1500 dozen ears. We got paid $1.50 a day plus our lunch and supper. It was $2 a day at harvest time when the work was harder.

My dad started raising mink that summer so that was another chore and learning experience.

1940 Armistice Day Storm, November 11

It was raining gently when I was 15 and stepped out on the open porch to have a better look at the weather. It looked like a perfect duck hunting day. Snuffy, our dog, was right behind me wondering what I was up to. I think Snuffy sensed that I should be in school. But when I went into the garage to get two or three decoys, there was no question about it. Snuffy knew what I was going to do. He got so excited he picked up a decoy to help me.

I looked at our duck boat to see if there was any way I could haul it or load it on my Model A Ford by myself. There wasn't, so I decided to hunt on the edge of the swamp.

Snuffy followed my steps where ever I went hoping we'd get going. I told Ma we were going to the Ferry Bridge on the way to Savage. I grabbed my warmest clothing, boots, mitts and the old blanket we used to warm a wet Snuffy when he retrieved a duck from the water.

Pa always said if your oil and water was up to snuff, you won't get into trouble, so I checked them and they were OK. I didn't have any Prestone Anti-freeze, so I took a small bucket along to dip into the swamp to replace the water when I was through hunting. The gas gauge showed two gallons.I hoped that would be enough. I opened the door and told Ma, "Snuffy and I are leaving. We won't be gone too long."

"Be careful. It's getting colder. It feels like it's going to snow."

"It's Okay, Ma. I have my warmest clothes on." Snuffy hopped in to sit right next to me.

We got to our hunting place just fine. But Ma was right. It was starting to snow and the wind was starting to pick up. Heavenly big flakes began to slush the swamp water and also cut our visibility. I buttoned my coat up to my neck and put my shells in my pants so I had room for my hands or my mittens in my coat pockets.

This storm was becoming serious. I didn't dare to put Snuffy in that cold slush. While I was trying to make up my mind about leaving, three ducks flew by so close they startled me.

"Come, Snuffy. We'd better get out of here while we still have a chance."

We headed the Model A for home and crossed the Ferry Bridge, but half way up the hill I spun out. I backed down the hill and tried it again. No luck. The rain we had had in the morning was now frozen ice under the snow. I could see I wasn't going to make it up the hill, so I had to go home the long way to Savage and then to Bloomington.

I managed to get to my friend Don Pearson's house and turned into his yard and parked the car and drained my water so the block wouldn't freeze. The gas gauge now showed empty. I didn't know if I could drive another couple of miles or not and I sure didn't want to be stranded in a snow drift. I tried calling our house, but the phones were out of order. After I visited a couple of hours with Don, I decided I'd better walk for home before it got dark. I bid Don farewell and said, "Let's go home, Snuff."

We just climbed up a gentle hill when Snuffy took a flip with all four feet. The wind had cleared the snow down to the bare road. Still, it wasn't extremely cold. I was dressed warmly enough. Snuffy and I didn't have any trouble walking home.

Ma wasn't there when we got home. She must have gone to the neighbors to see if their phone was working. Ma finally came home.

"Where's the car?"

"At Pearsons. It's almost out of gas. Where is supper, Ma?"

"Supper! You're worried about supper when I'm trying to call somebody to find out where you are!"

"Oh! Ma, don't get so excited."

"I've been listening to the radio. The snow plows have found people frozen to death. Some have burned their car cushions and tires too. Some duck hunters were frozen to death. One person was frozen close to where you went to hunt."

"Where is Pa?"

"Your dad managed to call. He expects to be home in two or three days." "I'm sorry Ma." (I don't really remember if I said that, but I should have.)

When the roads were open the highway plows found about sixty people who were frozen to death, some in Dakota and Wisconsin, too. The tragic part of this story was that, because it had been relatively warm weather that morning, people were caught unprepared.

1940 Runaway

What compelled Bruce, and later me and Alfred, to try to run away to Alaska? The times may have had more to do with it than anything else. Life in the 1930s wasn't easy. My pa worked long hours delivering beer and soft drinks and in the winter there were days when he made sixty stops and never sold a case.

My ma's days were equally tough, gardening and canning everything that could be preserved, including vegetables, fruit, venison, pork and chicken, trying to stay within four dollars a week. I think washing clothes was the hardest. Ma had to shave Fels-Naptha soap in the wash boiler and boil the dirty clothes and then transfer them with a stick to the wash tub to scrub on the wash board. It was a good time for Bruce and me to stay clear of the house.

Bruce and I put in long days in the summer also, gardening or working on neighboring farms. Having changed schools six times by the time we were in seventh grade didn't help – we were both having difficulty with school. Physical work was of more importance and it was what Bruce and I did the best. We were expected to do a man's job but we felt like we were treated like little kids. We wanted to prove that we were grown up and could be trusted to make good decisions by ourselves. So, we each ran away.

Alfred was agreeable when I suggested that maybe it was time for us to head west. I reminded Alfred of how my brother, Bruce, did it. Bruce had asked me to come along on his paper route, saying, "Details, Irvin, you must remember the details." I couldn't imagine why I needed to know the small stuff. It wasn't my paper route. When we returned home Bruce made the announcement that he was leaving, and that I had inherited the paper route. Bruce was going to Seattle, Washington, and from there ... Alaska was just across the water.

That's exactly what Alfred and I had in mind. I packed a gunnysack: clean underwear, socks, shirt, jeans, a knife, my Pa's 44 revolver, and some ammunition. I charged a few cans of beans on my parents' account. I didn't have any money, but then I was going to make a good living in Alaska.

At fifteen, I wasn't brave enough to say goodbye to my parents (and I was too worried that they'd try to stop me) so I left a note on the kitchen table:

Dear Mom & Dad I'm leaving home to go West. Don't worry about me. Love, Irvin

Alfred didn't beat around the bush with his mother. "Ma, I'm heading west with Irvin," he said.

"Take some clean underwear, Alfred," she replied calmly, probably suspecting we'd never make it. Good thing she mentioned the underwear because that was all that Alfred took.

Alfred and I planned to walk five miles to Savage, Minnesota and hop a train, without the slightest idea of when a train would come by. Alfred and I started to think about what we were doing. A train whistle in the distance dimmed our doubts. We were ready to sever our ties from Bloomington forever.

We crouched along the tracks and waited for the train to pass so we could jump on. The train, a forty mile-an-hour blur, never slowed down, and blasted the whistle at us as it sped past. Soon after, a second train came by and did the same thing. Undaunted, our spirits still high, we calculated a new plan: We were sure that trains must stop in Shakopee, a larger town ten miles farther away.

We walked the railroad tracks, stepping from tie to tie, sometimes trying to walk the rail, both very tiring. Once there, to pass the time, Alfred and I sat on the depot freight dock and ate a can of cold beans. At last, we heard the sweet sound of a train whistle in the distance. We quickly repacked our gunnysack and prepared to leave Minnesota forever.

Woosh-woo-woo-woosh. The train sped past. Alfred and I looked at each other in disbelief. We sat on the freight dock and talked about everything we could think of except, of course, defeat. The sky was pitch black now, and the notion of leaving Minnesota was taking on an entirely different perspective. Neither one of us wanted to be the first to suggest going home, even though we both wanted to.

"You know, Irv, my folks are getting kind of old," Alfred finally said. "I really think I should go back home to help them."

"Al, you're absolutely right. My folks are getting pretty old too. Let's go back." I threw the gunnysack on my shoulder, and Alfred and I headed down the tracks for home. We didn't talk much, and the gunnysack was starting to feel very heavy. I wished that I had never taken it.

"Why don't you chuck it?" Alfred asked.

"I'd better not," I replied nervously. "I'm in enough trouble already. If I chuck it, I'll really catch it." Alfred and I trudged on. Our energy was spent and we stumbled occasionally which added to our misery. We were beat. A large can of beans in the gunnysack was gouging me in the shoulder. Alfred got a large blister on one foot, so he limped alongside me, trying to favor the sore spot and not complain about it.

We parted company at the town hall. It was three a.m. When I arrived home, I quietly opened the unlocked door and put the gunnysack on the floor, loosened my belt to remove and put down my dad's revolver, and slipped out of my filthy clothes. I crawled into bed and within five seconds was dead to the world. That didn't last long.

"What's the meaning of all this?" my dad hollered in my ear as he flipped on the light and whipped off the covers. I blinked hard, hoping it was a dream or nightmare and that I hadn't really run away after all. But the gunnysack, sprawled on the floor with the contents scattered about, confirmed the truth.

"If you try that stunt again, don't bother coming back home!" my dad blurted out as he left, slamming the bedroom door behind him.

I managed to recover emotionally (and physically), went back to school, and chalked the incident up as a very difficult time in my life. I had learned a valuable lesson from this experience -- travel light and bring some MONEY.

1940 I Tried That Stunt Again

Several months later, Alfred and I again began plotting our escape to Alaska. I had five dollars in my pocket. Alfred and I bummed a ride to the Twin Cities, a place where we could hop a freight train. We traveled light, just a pocket knife and Alfred's barn shoes.

The train we wanted to catch was already on the move, traveling slowly until it got out of the Twin Cities. After Alfred put on his heavy barn shoes, we started running. I managed to get on the train and reached for Alfred's hand. Alfred dropped one of his school shoes. "What good is one shoe?" Alfred asked, as he tossed the other shoe away. We were so exuberant that we had managed to hop the train, we started singing "The Wabash Cannon Ball" at the top of our lungs.

It soon became very apparent that the boxcar we were riding had a flat wheel. The car pounded and vibrated, our stomachs tightened up into knots, and there wasn't any way to move to another car until the train stopped. It was a warm January in Minnesota, but when the sun went down, it was downright cold. We weren't singing anymore. The pounding of the car seemed to say "warm bed at home" again and again. After hundreds of miles, it was a very long night.

At daylight, Alfred and I squinted out the boxcar door wondering where we were. All we could see were prairie, fence posts, barbed wire and tumbleweeds. When the train pulled on a side track to let a passenger train pass, we seized our first opportunity and moved to another car, a coal gondola. After the train started moving again, we weren't so sure that this was the best choice either. The coal dust swirled around our heads like a cyclone, and it was much colder because of the wind.

We waited for the train to stop. At the first chance, we climbed up on top of the boxcar, which turned out to be the poorest choice we had made so far. For a hundred miles, we had to lay down and hang on for dear life. When we went through a tunnel, Alfred and I were certain that we were going to get scraped off or suffocate from the smoke. We were almost freezing to death.

On the postive side, we were gaining experience.

When the train finally stopped, and Alfred and I were able to talk again, I said, "You know, Al, I bet it's nice and warm right behind the engine on the coal tender." It was warmer all right, but I hadn't considered the sparks and cinders coming out of the stack. Every time the fireman opened the boiler door, a gusty draft made the sparks really fly. Alfred and I decided that we didn't want to burn to death either, so at the next opportunity we moved inside another boxcar with ROUND wheels.

The train stopped in Miles City, Montana, at a big railroad yard. Alfred remembered that his girlfriend Shirley had a cousin who moved to Miles City from Bloomington, where she went to school with us. "Let's go to her school and say hello," Alfred suggested. We found the high school and approached the door. Suddenly I took a good look at Alfred. All I could see were the whites of his eyes and his teeth. "Al, do I look as dirty as you do?" I asked. "She's not stuck up," Alfred reassured me. "Let's go in."

A surprised office secretary directed us to Shirley's cousin's classroom. We rapped on the door and a teacher hurried out. "You can't go in there," she said firmly. "They're taking a test." When Shirley's cousin finally came to the door, I didn't expect her to admit that she knew us.

She greeted us as old friends and offered to bring us home to meet her father. We were lucky that her mother wasn't home -- she probably wouldn't have given us such a warm reception. Alfred and I were famished, and Shirley's cousin cooked bacon, eggs and potatoes for us. As soon as the food caught up with our stomachs, we started to yawn. Shirley's cousin suggested we get some rest so we slept on the front floor for three hours. Shirley's cousin's dad tried to convince us to stay for the night, but we were both so filthy that we felt out of place.

It was time to head out into the darkness to figure out what we were going to do next. At the train yard, the guard told us there weren't any trains going west until morning. Restless to move forward, we stood by the side of the road and stuck out our thumbs.

A policeman pulled up. "What are you guys up to?" he asked.

"We're going to Cody, Wyoming," I answered.

"You boys won't get anywhere this time of night. Let me put you in the hoosegow til morning." The jail wasn't bad at all. There wasn't any mattress or blankets, but it was warmer than staying out all night.

Early in the morning, we headed for the railroad yard to select a decent boxcar to ride. The next stop was Cody, Wyoming. Alfred and I had used up most of the five dollars, but we had a plan. We would work in Cody long enough to get enough money to go on to Seattle. And from there ... well, Alaska was just across the water. Cody was warmer than usual for January. There wasn't much going on in this small town in mid-winter. Alfred knew farming and I had worked on farms, so we figured there must be some farm work that we could do. The local people grinned when we asked about work. They knew work was difficult (if not impossible) to come by in January.

At dusk, Alfred and I decided we'd better find a place to sleep. We hurried down the road toward the Shoshone River when we spotted a corral. Twenty horses milled about the corral, and a stack of hay was fenced off in the middle. Alfred and I felt our way through the darkness, trying not to rouse the horses. The horses nickered and blew their nostrils, but we managed to reach the stack of hay quietly. I'd seen pictures of bums sleeping in haystacks. That's what we were going to do. We frantically pulled out hay trying to make a hole large enough to crawl into and managed to make openings big enough for our bodies but not our shoulders. In about thirty minutes, our shoulders felt like ice, and we gave up the haystack idea.

Alfred and I moved to a bridge that we had sighted earlier. There was a lot of loose hay on the edge of the bridge. We gathered it together to take underneath the bridge so that we could make a nest. The hay insulated us from the ground. We slept close together, covered with the hay. By three a.m., we were sound asleep. It started raining. Water dripped off the bridge and by daybreak, the hay was soaked. Alfred and I miserably looked for dry sticks to make a fire. With the fire crackling and the aroma of wood smoke, and fresh outdoors, we soon forgot about the unpleasant night.

Alfred noticed a tar paper shack nearby. A dim light cast a glow in the window and soon a swirl of smoke came out of the smoke stack. The screen door squeaked and an old man came outside to take a leak. The man disappeared back into the shack. He seemed not to notice us. Thirty minutes later, the screen door squeaked again, and this time the old man came towards us.

"Good morning, boys," he said. "Come to my cabin. I've got coffee and hotcakes." The old man, Tom Russell, was friendly and made us feel welcome. Alfred wolfed down the hotcakes so fast that I nudged him in the ribs.

"Slow up," I whispered, "or this guy will never feed us again." Alfred and I stayed on with Tom.

After a few days Alfred started complaining. There wasn't any work around, and he was beginning to miss Shirley immensely. "You can go home, Alfred, " I said flatly, "but I'm staying." And that's exactly what Alfred did. I had the feeling that I wasn't getting anywhere either, but I wasn't ready to give up.

Tom's income came from cleaning out the Silver Dollar Saloon once a week for two dollars. I noticed he always wore his overshoes the day that he worked. It didn't seem to matter if it was rain or shine. One night when Tom came home from work I watched him take a bottle of liquor out of his overshoes. I asked about this and Tom said that he always poured a little whiskey, brandy, gin or whatever was open on the back bar, into two empty bottles, careful never to take enough from the bottle that it would be noticed. He said it helped make up for the low pay.

Tom and I both worked at the dump picking up scrap metal, mostly copper wire scraps along the powerline. I shot rabbits with Tom's 22 rifle and I shot suckers in the river, easy to see when the water was low. I unloaded hay at a slaughterhouse. In exchange for my work, the storekeeper always gave me bacon butts, and sometimes other meat trimmings. Even a jar of honey was a special treat. When I was home, I didn't like honey, but now I craved something sweet.

One day, I admitted that Alfred was right. At this rate, I'd never make enough money to go on to Seattle. It was time to go back home. I washed my clothes. My underwear were now threadbare and offered practically no warmth. From the Silver Dollar, where the sheepherders shed clothes they had worn for six months without washing them, Tom brought clothes home. That was how I aquired a pair of jeans. The storekeeper had also given me two pair of light canvas gloves. I stopped by the Silver Dollar to bid farewell to Tom. He wasn't around, so I left words of good-bye and thanks for him.

The trains stopping in Cody didn't have a regular schedule because Cody was off the main railroad track. It was early afternoon, so I decided not to wait for a train and headed off on foot. The temperature was dropping and big snowflakes fell from the sky. A few miles out of Cody, it was a full-scale blizzard. I couldn't see more than a few feet in front of me, and not a single car had passed me yet. I walked briskly, my burlap gunnysack full of meager belongings helping to keep me warm.

I spotted headlights in the distance. *Please*, I pleaded, *whoever you are, please stop and give me a ride.* The car did stop, and a Morman priest going to Powell, close to the Wyoming /Montana stateline, gave me a lift. When he dropped me off, he gave me fifteen cents and wished me a lot of luck.

It had quit snowing, but the temperature continued to drop. I walked on and was about a mile out of town when another car stopped to see if I wanted a ride. I jumped in. "How far east you going?" the man asked.

"To Minneapolis," I answered.

The man stopped the car. "I'm sorry, son, but you'll have to go back to Powell and take the other road out of town. This road is closed for the winter going through the mountains."

Regretfully, I climbed out of the car and started walking back to Powell. It was getting dark again. I went into the pool hall to warm up a bit. Nervously, I began to place up and down the few blocks of Powell trying to keep warm and decide what to do. I passed by a small hotel, with just a dozen rooms, on each stroll. About the fourth pass, a small man came out to ask if I had a place to stay for the night. I didn't, but I was too leery to go with him, so I insisted that I was okay. The impact of traveling alone began to sink in. I'd heard several horror stories about things that had happened to boys traveling by themselves.

Alone with Friends

"Don't be afraid of me," the man said. "I have a big Norwegian partner. You'll like him." Reluctantly, I decided to go with the man.

I was bigger than he was, and I didn't think that he could harm me physically. Of course, I wasn't sure about his partner, but I was very cold and decided to take my chances. The man took me to his place, a small empty store building with sparse furnishings, just a table and three chairs.

Then, the Norwegian showed up. The two men prepared supper and gave me the largest portion of meat. I knew then they were genuinely concerned about my welfare. After we ate, they apologized for not having a bed. They said they had had a beautiful brass bed, but they had to sell it when times were tough. The mention of a brass bed brought Tom Russell back to mind. I rather missed the old coot.

Tom's friend, Bill, had mentioned a beautiful brass bed once when we were junking.

"Irv, your eyes would bug out if you saw that bed," Bill said. Bill hauled scrap, stuff that was too heavy for Tom or me to carry. One time when I was with Bill, the rear end of his truck locked up from the heavy weight. Bill called a friend to tow the truck to Tom's shack.

"What do I owe ya?" Bill asked his friend.

"One dollar will be enough."

Tom and Bill looked at me. They knew I had a silver dollar, and it was the first silver dollar that I'd ever seen. I was saving it to bring back to Minnesota someday, but I paid the towing bill because I'd already learned that survival meant helping each other.

To my amazement, this big Norwegian and the small man knew Bill too. They had been partners with him for a long time.

"Bill's in town now. We'll go find him," the little fellow offered.

Soon, they returned with Bill. Bill and I talked about Tom and lots of other things. When Bill asked me where I was sleeping, I told him these two guys had said I could stay with them.

"I have a better place for you to sleep," Bill said. I followed him to a little house near the edge of town. "This is where you're sleeping tonight, Irv." The house was nice and warm. Bill told me to sleep by the stove and that he'd be back about five in the morning. I don't know where Bill slept, but at five o'clock he was back to wake me up.

"Whose house did I sleep in?" I asked.

"Friends," Bill answered simply. "I didn't want to wake them up."

Bill charged my breakfast at the restaurant. I tried to give Bill the one dollar that Don Pearson gave to me, betting that I wouldn't stay a month at Cody, but he wouldn't take it.

"My credit's good here, isn't it Charley?" Bill yelled over to the cook.

"You bet," the cook replied, much to Bill's relief. I took the fifteen cents that the priest gave me and bought Bill a cigar. It was time for me to move on.

Hitch-Hiking

Back on the road, it was getting windy and colder. The farther I walked, the colder I got. I walked as fast as I could, putting my hands together to try to keep them warm. After a couple of miles, a pickup truck finally came by.

"Young man, I've never picked up a hitchhiker before," the rancher said, "but I couldn't pass you up in such nasty weather. You're going to freeze to death out here!" Ten miles later, the rancher stopped the pickup truck.

"Sorry, Son, this is where I turn off. Good luck."

As I walked I pounded my feet and patted my hands together, praying for the next car to come along. It sure seemed like I was miles from anywhere warm. A few miles later, a black 1939 Ford sedan screeched to a halt beside me.

"Hop in," the guy yelled. What a break. This car was nice and warm, even though the owner drove like a lunatic. He explained that he was a cattle buyer, with a lot of miles to drive, and that he was always in a hurry. Twenty or thirty miles later, he stopped the car.

"Sorry, kid, but I've got to turn off here. If you're on the road when I come back, I'll pick you up." And with that, he was off.

Shoot-- I'd hoped that I'd be left in a town, but at least I was continually moving East. It was dark when the cattle buyer had left me alongside the road. It felt like thirty degrees below zero, and I knew the wind chill was even colder.

I continued to trudge along all night. Towards morning, I had slowed down so much that I thought that I was going to freeze to death. But I knew I shouldn't be far from Laurel, Montana. I decided that if I saw a house, I would knock on the door and tell them that I was literally freezing to death. Finally, I spotted a lone house on the prairie in the distance. I calculated that I had to make it another mile.

I was within yards of the house when a panel truck stopped. The man asked if I wanted a ride. I was so stiff that I could barely get into the truck. Inside, I sat back and let the heater blast hot air on me. What a luxury. The driver told me that he delivered baked goods to Laurel. We weren't far from Laurel, just a few miles. When we arrived at his first stop, I had to get out and woefully leave the heater. I felt like I was starving to death, too.

"Do you have any old rolls?" I asked the delivery man as I climbed out of the truck. "Nah, it's too early." Reaching into the back of the truck, he grabbed a fresh package of rolls and handed them to me with a smile. The delivery man would never know how much these rolls meant to me that particular morning.

Riding the Rail

It was still dark, and everything was covered with snow. I headed for the railroad yard. I couldn't find any sticks to build a fire with. I watched the passenger dining car go by. The passengers drank hot coffee and ate. I could almost taste hash browns, sausages, and toast. I ate one of my rolls. It was real and tasted pretty good.

The small engine waited in the switch yard. I watched the engine go back-and-forth, occasionally sitting still for a while. I noticed a small fire. A trainman had pulled a hotbox, oil-saturated cotton waste used for lubrication around a wheel bearing. The waste got too hot and caught on fire. I was huddled there for warmth when the engineer of the switch engine called me over to warm up in his cab. I had to get out when it was time for him to switch again. The engineer pointed out that there weren't any trains going East until the next day.

My brother Bruce had told me that some of the yards had a sand house. Each train engine has a sand hopper with a tube to direct the sand to the track if the train can't get traction. I tried to spot a building that matched the description: a building that has a boiler fenced in with sand so that the sand will dry. When I found it, I spread out on the warm sand and fell asleep.

When I woke up, a bum was sleeping on the sand next to me. He was an older man, and the only person I'd met that was riding the rods in the northern rail belt. He woke up and asked me how "bumming" was down the trail. I told him that I didn't know because I hadn't tried it. He was quick to tell me that he wouldn't work for a handout.

The old man's hands were so scaled with dirt that I felt sorry for him. He complained that his hands were cold. I dug into my burlap bag and gave him my extra work gloves. He turned the gloves this way and that, examining them thoroughly.

"Sure are flimsy," the bum muttered. "And, they don't look very warm." I felt like grabbing the gloves back, but I didn't. I said good-bye to the ungrateful old jigger.

I managed to get a ride all the way to Billings, Montana, only to discover that there weren't any trains going East from there that day either. Since hitchhiking had been going well, I thumbed another ride all the way to Miles City.

In Miles City, I hurried to the railroad yard to see if a train was getting ready to head East. The railroad men were just going on shift. I ran to catch up with one of them. "Is this train going East today?" I asked.

"Yes, it is," the railroad man said abruptly, and he kept on walking. He walked down the track a little ways and then he turned back to me.

"You're not going to try to take it, are you?" he asked.

"Yes, I am," I said, wondering why I shouldn't take it.

"You'll freeze to death," the man said bluntly. "I guess you might as well freeze going East as here. I'll try to find you a decent car. Don't follow me too close; I'm not supposed to help you." The railroad man looked up and down the full length of the train. All the boxcars were sealed. He pointed to a car.

"Take that flatbed with the big square timbers. It's the only safe car because the timbers shouldn't shift," he said quickly, and then he walked away. I went to the flatbed and found some heavy paper to wrap around my body to keep the wind from penetrating my clothes. Soon the train was rolling and I was beginning to think that I really could make it back to Minnesota.

When we stopped to let a passenger train pass, the railroad man came running down the track to check me. "How ya doing, kid?" he hollered.

"I'm fine." I answered quickly.

"What's your name, anyway?" the man asked.

"Irvin," I replied, surprised at his interest.

"Okay, Irvin, hang in there. I'll check on you later," and the man disappeared again. For several stops the man came to check on me. "How ya doing, Irv?"

"Okay," I'd reply.

Finally the railroad man came running down the tracks shouting, "Get out of there, Irv. I'm going to let you ride in the caboose. My partner gets off here."

As we walked back to the caboose, the man continued to talk rapidly. "My partner would have reported me if I let you ride in the caboose while he was in there. But if you would have started freezing, I would have let you ride with me regardless."

I found comfort in the stranger's words. I sacked out near the red-hot potbellied stove and fell asleep. It seemed like only five minutes when the man was already waking me up.

"You got to get out, Irv. This shift is over. I've got to leave now."

I hated to get out, but I didn't have any choice. I was still chilled to the bone and began to wonder if I had hypothermia. I simply wasn't warming up. I went back to the flatbed and wrapped myself in paper. I was just getting tucked in when my railroad friend came with a quart of hot coffee and six donuts. I appreciated his concern and told him so. He gave me a paper with his name and address. "Would you mind dropping me a note to let me know you made it?"

"Sure I will," I promised. As the railroad man shook my hand, the train started moving.

"Good luck, Irv," he shouted above the roar.

The next day, I didn't know where I was: Montana? Dakota? The train that I'd been riding was staying wherever we were. I had to get on another train. I tried to remember the tricks that Bruce had told me about riding the rail: don't get trapped in a reefer car; don't ride in a gondola with lumber because it shifts; don't try to catch a moving train by grabbing the rear of a car.

Bruce had advice about getting food. *If you're hungry and have a little money, buy one onion, one carrot, one potato, and ask the storekeeper if he has a bone. Chances are he'll give you a little piece of meat. Go to the bakery and ask for a dime's worth of stale rolls. Chances are the baker will give you a sack full.* I decided to try the bakery trick. I had a long wait for the next train because it was a doubleheader that had to be prepared to climb a big hill. I went to the bakery and asked for a dime's worth of stale rolls. I did get a sack full. I went to a restaurant, ordered coffee and ate several.

I went back to the train yard to pick a car to ride in. I selected an empty boxcar. The train started moving very slowly. It was a very long train. It took a long time to get up any speed.

When the train was climbing the hill, I was shocked to see an arm reaching into the boxcar. An older man struggled to climb on board. Instinctively, I reached for his arm and helped him. He expressed that he was very grateful.

"You must be a Finlander," I said smiling.

"How did you know?" the man asked.

"You sound like one," I answered with a laugh.

We enjoyed talking. The man said he traveled the rail for fun and that when he got tired, he'd rent a room and rest up. He was very fortunate to have that option. He wasn't a bum. He just enjoyed the excitement of this kind of travel. He had on new bib overalls, a new wool mackinaw, and other fine quality clothing. It was fun to visit with a Finn, like me, and not just another bum. But my Finlander friend rode about one hundred miles, and I was alone again.

The train stopped in a large city in the Dakotas. It was very late at night, and I went to the passenger train depot to warm up. I started to open the door and was stopped by a bulky man who said briskly, "We don't allow bums in here." He was the first railroad bull that I encountered. I left quickly, thinking *I look like a bum.*

I stomped my feet and beat my hands, trying to warm up. With plenty of time to find another car to ride in, and figuring the bull was warm inside and not likely to be out freezing in the yard, I began my search. All the boxcars were sealed, but I found a gondola with a load of small lumber and eight empty feet on one end. I knew it was dangerous, but I didn't have any choice.

I waited and hoped this one would go all the way to Minneapolis. There was room to walk around and I was grateful for that. I walked, and walked, trying to keep warm. I became exhausted and decided to rest. I put my feet in some empty cement sacks and put my hands between my legs and sat on a 5 gallon can. I fell asleep. I awoke to the crash of a 2x6 which missed my chest by inches. I was frightened and that was the end of my sleeping.

Thinking of Home

The train pulled into Minneapolis at three a.m. and traveled slowly through the city. I wasn't sure where to jump off, but I wanted to be near a road that went home to Bloomington. I could barely believe that I had made it this far. I jumped off into the darkness, tumbling in the cinders but not getting hurt.

As I walked along, searching for a street what was familiar, I thought of home (really thought of "home") for the first time. Dad's words echoed in my mind. *Next time you get a notion like this, don't bother coming home!* Did he really mean it?

I saw a light in a small restaurant. Peeking in the window, I saw a man mixing hotcake batter. "Is it too early for breakfast?" I asked as I walked in.

"No," he said, throwing me a puzzled look.

"Can I get a cup of coffee and a hotcake for fifteen cents?" It was all the money that I had left.

"Sure," the cook replied. "Kid, why don't you go wash up? You'll feel better."

In the washroom, I realized how lousy I looked. My face was windburned and saturated with coal dust and God knows what else. I tried to wash, but it hurt when I touched my face. I felt a little better when I returned to the table. I had a stack of hotcakes and coffee waiting for me. I thanked the cook exuberantly because he gave me far more than fifteen cents worth.

My steps lightened the last few miles, but I still wondered what kind of reception I'd get at home. I spotted Pa's gray 1935 Ford coming down the road toward me. I figured he was on his way to work at about 6:30 a.m. I jumped behind a tree. I wasn't ready to face Pa yet. He passed by without seeing me. When I finally walked in the front door at home, Ma took a look at me.

"You sure look tired and hungry, Irvin." No hug. She had a pot of stew on the stove and dished up a helping for me.

"Ma, this sure is good," I said. "Why didn't you make it like this when I was home?"

She looked at me and grinned. "That's the kind you don't like, Irvin."

When Pa got home from work, he took one look and said, "Did you get the bus ticket, Irvin?" Bus ticket? Aw, shucks. Thinking of the experiences on my own way home, I was glad that I didn't get the ticket. I probably wouldn't have used it anyway.

ALASKA'S CALL

1941 North to Alaska

"What are your plans now, Irvin?" Pa asked. It was a legitimate question.

"I don't know," I replied. It was a legitimate answer.

Go to school? I wasn't exactly bursting with qualifications for any particular job. For a few days, I dealt with the simple questions and avoided the greater issues. I came across the scrap of paper from the railroad man. I wrote him a letter telling him that I had made it after all and thanked him for helping me. At least he'd know that I didn't freeze to death going East.

I ran into Alfred's brother. Alfred's brother wasn't sure of the details, but he did know that Alfred had just returned from another attempt at fleeing Minnesota. He went South and ended up picking fruit to survive. I decided it was a good time to pay Alfred a visit.

Alfred was thin, filthy, unshaven, and sleeping on the couch. I figured he couldn't have been home too long because he hadn't even cleaned up yet. I peered closer to be certain it was him. Then I remembered what I looked like the morning I returned from Cody, scarcely recognizing my image in the restaurant washroom mirror. I poked Alfred with my finger a few times. He finally opened his eyes and grinned at me in a sleepy haze.

"Irv, you should have been there," Alfred said dreamily. "It was a real bumming trip."

That settled it. The only way I was ever going to Alaska was to get a real job that paid real money and save up enough to make the trip. Runaway trips for young boys without money was a circle tour that ended up right back home in Minnesota.

It wasn't a difficult decision not to go back to school. My educational pursuits hadn't been going all that well before I left home. I fell behind in Algebra, and I didn't relish the struggle that would lie ahead of me. Algebra and many other high school studies seemed irrelevant to the world. I never fit in with the rest of the crowd anyway because of my quiet nature. I was always on the outside looking in. Anxious to grow up, I wanted to get a job and make some money. I began to look for a job, any kind of job, to be able to earn the money I needed to get to Alaska, where I believed a promising future awaited me.

Pa was pleased that I'd decided to seek employment. He didn't want me hanging around resting up for another escapade. Pa would have liked me to finish school, but he understood I was anxious to begin working. He liked my ideas until I got to the part about Alaska.

Repeatedly, I would ask, "Pa, why can't we go homesteading in the Matanuska Valley?" It would have made it so much easier if he'd just agreed to pack up the family and go. But, instead, Pa kept reminding me that homesteading (as I planned to do in Alaska) would be very difficult.

"Irvin, let me tell you a bit about homesteading," Pa said patiently, hoping to inspire some sense. He told me about my great-grandpa, Hekki Savineimi, who came to the United States from Finland, settled in Michigan but soon gravitated to the Finnish settlement of New York Mills, Minnesota. Hekki wanted to homestead a piece of land. Everybody advised him to go East. Hekki arranged for his wife, Greta Savineimi, and their children to stay with friends in New York Mills while he searched for land to homestead. My grand-father Bill Savineimi, Hekki's son, worked on the railroad and helped with the farm work. When my grandfather was eighteen, he married a lovely girl named Situnia. They lived on Hekki's homestead and produced two fine sons, my father John and my uncle Eddie. (When my father was five years old, the family decided to change their name from Savineimi to Savela. Everyone agreed but Greta, who remained a Savineimi until the day she died.)

My grandparents, Bill and Situina, wanted a homestead of their own, and following in his father's footsteps, Bill decided to go North with his wife and two sons to homestead a parcel. He wanted to be away from his parents and their now very well-established homestead. The nearby railroad went to Graceton, Minnesota, and Bill decided to homestead land near there. At first Bill was disappointed in the swampy land on his homestead. Then he realized there would always be deer in that wild country and nobody would be able to homestead South of him.

"Situnia, when times get better, it would be nice to buy some dynamite. I could sure make time on those stumps then." But the good times never came, as far as money was concerned. As the boys grew, Eddie ran errands and my uncle Raynold, their third child and my namesake, helped with the stump work. Cash income was rare. The only chance to make money was if a mill was being constructed in the area and lumber was needed. Sometimes, Bill and John hopped a freight train with other homesteaders and worked in the harvest fields of the Dakotas. My father John, just twelve years old, was paid a man's wages because he did a man's job. When Bill and Situnia were blessed with another child, baby Julia, Bill decided it was time to raise the family's standard of living. He left the homestead and obtained work on the Mesabi Iron Range. As the years passed Bill returned to farm around Sebeka.

My father hadn't forgotten a single thing about those early years, homesteading with his family near Graceton, Minnesota.

"Irvin, I'm so fortunate to have a steady job," Pa continued. "I can't give up that security to begin another homesteading adventure. I've been there, and I don't want to go back. I hope you'll give serious thought to what I've told you today."

Although many Minnesotans were leaving Minnesota at this time to go to Russia in search of a better life, Pa wasn't convinced that going North was the answer. He reminded me about my great-uncle who went to Russia. Through the grapevine, we heard that my great-uncle who had gone to Russia was killed there. It wouldn't have surprised me or the other relatives any because my great-uncle was always very outspoken about his thoughts. But I wasn't convinced that Alaska wasn't the place for me, with or without my parents. Alaska was calling me. I kept my thoughts about homesteading to myself, never abandoning the idea.

Pa worked at a soft drink company, and he heard about a truck driving job for a helper to deliver beer in the Twin Cities. You had to be a licensed driver. Since I was, I rushed to apply for the job. I was happy to get it, and I worked hard, eager to earn the paycheck and save my money to go North. I soon found out that saving money was an incredibly slow process.

President Roosevelt announced over the radio that Japan had bombed Pearl Harbor, December 7, 1941, and my dream of going to Alaska started to sprout. Several boys and I scurried over to the Army and Navy headquarters to see if we could join up. Of course, at sixteen and seventeen years old we were all too young.

1942 National Youth Association (NYA)

Then I discovered the National Youth Association (NYA) and my days of driving the beer truck were over. Actually, they were over sooner than I expected. I was laid off. I was astounded that I'd been hired because the company needed someone to help during vacation relief. It was a not-so-grand introduction into what can happen in the world of grown-up work. But, the NYA soon helped me forget my employment troubles. I enrolled in welding school and was too busy going to classes for eight hours a day to give the truck driving job thought.

Our welding instructors were skilled tradesmen who knew every aspect of their craft. For the first time, I felt like my life was taking a positive twist. After school hours, we were given four-hour work assignments, and NYA students worked on the roads, served food, and worked in the mess halls, cleaned the latrines, worked in the boiler room, or worked on the NYA farm.

The NYA paid us $8 a month and gave us room and board. For clothing, we were given World War I hobnailed shoes, shirts, and pants. I felt lucky to be a part of the program. I studied and worked hard, anxious to prove that I was worthy of being chosen.

Three months later, I passed the Navy test. That was my ultimate ticket to head North. The NYA sent me by train to Seattle, along with other welding students who had passed the Navy test, to work as an apprentice welder in the shipyards. It was a different train ride than the one I'd experienced in the boxcars to and from Cody. This time I was an authorized passenger.

The fresh group of Minnesota welding students arrived in Seattle and were placed in the NYA camp to resume welding classes. As Midwesterners, we found plenty of new experiences. We shared our quarters with young men from the Southern states and were amused by their expressions and unfamiliar dialogue. The Southern students snickered at our "accents."

But another, even more pleasant, surprise was girls in our welding classes. Several girls, about our ages, peered out from beneath welding hoods. The first time I saw them, I tried to conceal my astonishment. Female welders—I hadn't even considered such a wonderful possibility.

The only problem was that the girls were housed at a different facility. The boys never got to see them except in welding class which put a crimp on the socializing with our feminine counterparts. Many of these women were later placed on major welding projects in the shipyards to relieve younger men to enter the service.

We young welders from Minnesota thought we were pretty good. After all, we had passed the Navy test. While in welding school in Minnesota, our main goal had been to master the vertical weld. The instructor thought if you could do the most difficult weld, you could learn the other positions with little difficulty. It still took a lot of practice and patience. The NYA welding school showed us that we had much to learn before we could be turned loose in a shipyard. The welding machines we had become accustomed to in Minnesota were different from the machines in Seattle. And it was wartime. We were taught to be very frugal with materials.

Welding rods were different in the Pacific Northwest. Some of the scrap metal we practiced on didn't respond the same as it had in Minnesota. Every bit of a welding rod had to be used, no exception. If the instructor noticed stubs with merely a half-inch of flux, he'd gather them together, bring them to our welding bench, and insist we finish using them correctly. In order to avoid the offending stubs on the welding bench, and the anguish of trying to make a nice weld while having to break the arc every few seconds, we quickly learned to be conservative.

When the instructor thought we were ready for the shipyard, he authorized us for private housing. As NYA welding students, we had been fairly sheltered from Seattle's atmosphere. The city was in a state of panic. People by the thousands arrived daily to help with the war effort. It was so crowded that it was difficult to find a place to stay. Every available room was being solicited for the influx of people arriving on the West coast. It certainly wasn't the city that I expected it to be. I registered at a housing program that encouraged the residents of Seattle to open their homes to workers. Two of my welding classmates and I were placed in a private home far away from the shipyards, an hour bus trip each way.

The NYA told us we had to join the boilermaker's union before we would be hired at the shipyard. The day I joined, I stood in line with prospective workers waiting to sign up at the Associated Shipyards. I shuffled my feet and waited, taking interest in two men in front of me. They were from the Philippines, and I couldn't understand a word they said. They spoke rapidly in their native language, and it didn't take me very long to figure out that they were discussing the application. I didn't know for sure what there were talking about, but I decided to follow my instinct and ask if they needed help with the application.

"Yes!" they quickly responded in unison. There was plenty of time to help get the papers completed as we waited to eventually reach the front of the line. Finally it was their turn to register, and I was relieved to see them have no problem getting signed up to work at the shipyards. When they finished, the two men stood off to one side, waiting patiently for me to finish. I walked over to them when I was done.

"Do you like Chinese food?" one of the men asked in broken English. They were extremely grateful that I had helped them and wanted to buy me dinner.

"Sure," I replied quickly, surprised at the invitation. The men took me to an authentic Chinese restaurant. I didn't know what to order and let the men order for me. The meal was served with chopsticks. When I had difficulty with the chopsticks, one of the men asked the waiter to bring me a fork. I was the only person in the restaurant who didn't look Oriental, and certainly the only one using a fork. It was an enjoyable dinner, and I thanked the men for their generosity. They felt I had earned my dinner by helping them with something they saw as very difficult.

The next day, after my first hour bus ride to work, I reported to my new job and was introduced to the foreman and a welding instructor. The foreman showed me to my new work assignment. As a "tacker" for two ship-fitters, my job was to weld an L-shaped piece of metal whenever one of the ship-fitters wanted it. The ship-fitter would drive a wedge under the L-shaped piece to force the metal plates together. If we had a problem, help was available from the instructor.

Every so often, I sensed someone watching me. The instructor would be standing alongside me, welding hood down, peering at how things were going. If the instructor was pleased, he would tell the foreman who would place us on a "jig" table to do some genuine welding. If a worker continued to do very good welding, he qualified as a journeyman and pay was increased.

I passed through the steps until I was moved from the jig table to work on the bottom of the ship, in the bow section. I liked welding, but welding on galvanized plates on the bow section was lousy. The ships were sub-chasers, and the bow section was made of two one-inch thick plates that were tough enough to ram a sub. It was difficult to breathe the smoke and fumes from the galvanized metal, even though suction tubes were supposed to pull out the smoke and fumes. Most of the smoke and fumes reached my face long before it reached the tubes.

I was disappointed in Seattle. I hated the crowds and the long bus rides. It was an hour commute each way, standing both ways on the bus. When we arrived downtown on the regular city transit bus, we had to transfer to a shipyard bus. The shipyard busses were old, dilapidated vehicles taken out of retirement to help haul the flood of workers to the shipyards during wartime. The shipyard bus was constant confusion. Many drivers were new to Seattle and didn't know one street from another. If someone asked to be let off on a certain street, the bus driver would say briskly, "Just tell me when we get there!" Often, there was a group of rowdy workers aboard who heckled the driver. Once, the driver was so frustrated with the verbal abuse that he stopped the bus in the middle of the block and refused to move until everyone became quiet. The busses were always crowded and the drivers asked passengers to step back, even when there wasn't room. Once when the bus was loaded to capacity, I saw a worker pull his friend in through a window at the rear of the bus. With plenty of time during the rides, I worked on ideas to get away from the congestion of Seattle and get across the water to Alaska. I still didn't have much money, but I desperately needed a change.

One day, I went to the employment office to see if there was any work I could do in Alaska. They sent me to a company which was hiring. I filled out the application, and everything was going very well until the lady came to my age.

"Sorry, we can't hire a seventeen year old kid," she said flatly. My mouth dropped. I was devastated. As I was leaving, an employee whispered, "Try E.W. Elliott Company, kid. I think they'll hire you."

I hurried to the E.W. Elliott Company and filled out another application before I lost my courage. The lady checked it carefully, while I held my breath. At last, she smiled and said, "We can hire you as a laborer working at Whitehorse, Yukon Territory, Canada."

I was so excited that I didn't even realize that I had no idea where Whitehorse, Yukon Territory, Canada was. The lady sent me to another desk to fill out a form for photo identification.

"It has to be green or blue," a girl behind the desk said clearly as she reviewed my form. "Your eyes," she said. "They have to be green or blue."

"They're hazel," I replied matter-of-factly.

"They can't be. They have to be green or blue," she said firmly. The girl examined my eyes, peering into them from six inches away. "I can't decide. Just a minute," she added. She motioned a couple of girls over to take a look. I blushed so much that I'm sure it affected my eye color. The girls giggled when I left the office, and I wasn't sure what color they finally settled on. I wondered how many guys had to pass their little eye test. But, it didn't matter. I was HIRED to work in Alaska and that was all that was important.

I was too young to go in the service and too young to get a regular job. The Canadian and United States government had signed the agreement to construct the Alaska Highway on March 6, 1942. It was my birthday. I was born for the Great Alaska Highway.

I had to quit my job at the shipyards and prepare to travel North. I needed a release from my job, but the foreman was reluctant to give me one.

"I'll quit anyway," I told him determinedly.

"You can't," the foreman threatened. "I'll have you put in the Army."

"Go ahead," I replied. It wasn't my nature to argue with a boss, but I knew I was on solid ground. Nobody was going to stop me. "I'm not old enough for the Army," I added calmly.

"Okay, kid. You win," the foreman said impatiently. He signed the release papers and let me go.

I gave up my room, knowing that some other worker would be very happy to get it. But I needed a place to stay for one more night. One of my welding classmates worked nights and offered his bed for that night.

I sent home most of the money I had earned, keeping a crisp $20.00 bill in my pocket to hold me until payday on my new job. Then I reported to the pier just as I'd been instructed to do. I had no sooner arrived when an announcement was made that the ship we were going to board had hit a log and was being repaired.

My affairs suddenly became complicated. My friend's landlady had questioned me about sleeping there the night before. I wouldn't admit to her that I had slept in my friend's bed, and I was afraid to go back for fear she'd find out the truth. I'd already dribbled away some of my money for food. Seattle didn't have five-cent hamburgers like Minnesota. I walked the streets of Seattle anxiously. I decided to spend the night in an all-night movie house. In the twilight of the indoor theatre, I endured crude comments and blue air all night, but the price was right.

The next day, I reported back to the pier to see if the boat was ready to set sail. The girl said it would be at least two more days. TWO MORE DAYS. How could I make my money last that long? For two more days, I walked the streets of Seattle, went to cheap movies, and ate cheap food. Two days later, I reported back to the pier.

When the girl again said it would be TWO MORE DAYS, I froze in my shoes. My money was gone, except for a $2.00 bill, the first

$2.00 bill I'd ever seen. I told this girl the truth: I was broke, and that I didn't have any place to stay.

"Why didn't you tell me this sooner!" she exclaimed. "All the men we hired to leave on this ship have been staying in a hotel with meals. The hotel even has a swimming pool! Young man, you should have spoken up." I kicked myself a few times for not asking about it sooner. Darn! The girl directed me to the hotel. I was able to stay in luxury for only one night. The following day the announcement came that the ship was ready to set sail.

Spirits were high among us new employees that morning. A large breakfast was served at the hotel, and I ate like I hadn't eaten in a week. It was the first good meal I'd had since I'd given up my room. After breakfast, a bus arrived to transport us to the wharf. On the way to the ship, the problems of the last week in Seattle began to vanish. I relaxed and was filled with exhilaration at the adventure of finally going North to Alaska.

A murmur of appreciation swept over the group of forty-six men when we pulled up to the pier. Before us stood a beautiful yacht. The Alician, a yacht owned by a millionaire, was leased to the E.W. Elliott Company to transport the employees to Skagway. Nobody dreamed we would be transported in such style. The Alician was breathtaking, 121 feet long and as sleek as a swordfish. Now, I was really excited, and for good reason. My first experience on a seagoing vessel was going to be truly magnificent. Two old-timers from Alaska had experienced this type of travel before so they weren't as eager as the rest of us. But for most of the men, this was a first experience they weren't likely to forget.

On the gangplank, a uniformed officer greeted us and welcomed us aboard. He gave the group brief instructions for we were passengers aboard "his" vessel. He stressed that we must set our footlockers and suitcases down gently so we wouldn't damage the deck. He wanted to keep the vessel as beautiful as it was. The Alician was impeccably clean, painted bright white except for the exposed dark teak 1 ½" slats divided by 1/4" of waterproof caulking. The contrast was elegant. The interior was finished just as grandly as the exterior with solid wood varnished panels polished to a glimmering sparkle. Our quarters were just off the officers' salon. The rooms were adequate but sparse, quickly identifying them as a temporary wartime necessity. In peacetime, I know this elegant ship had seen many affluent passengers. There were a large number of private cabins, a galley and a dining room. The dining room required two shifts to accommodate the large group of employees and crew members.

On a cool October day, excitement and curiosity heightened as the vessel glided smoothly through the turquoise water up the Inside Passage to Alaska. The men stood on the deck hoping to sight a whale or some other sea life and weren't disappointed. Whales and porpoises jumped in and out of the water, often diving in unison.

Sometimes, the weather was rainy and foggy, but for the most part, we could easily see tree-covered snow-capped mountains. After Seattle's pace, I felt like I finally could breathe easy again. I felt like a millionaire.

The crew ran the ship around us while we sipped hot coffee on the deck, watched the beautiful scenery, and swapped stories. As the youngest member of the group, I listened more than I talked. Most of the men were in their mid-thirties or older, well past draft age with a backlog of experience. Many of the men were from Minnesota, but several were from other places, such as the smoke jumper from Montana and the baker from Cordova. I didn't realize what a fine friend the baker would become in the future when I needed good conversation and something warm and sweet for my stomach. Many of the men were well-educated, particularly one man from Kansas who had attended medical school. His conversations were far more involved than the rest of the discussions. But, the baker from Cordova stood one-to-one with him.

The baker was an avid reader who would say modestly, "Yes, I've read quite a bit on the subject." He could discuss almost any subject in extraordinary detail, and we all enjoyed listening to these two men converse.

We discussed the reasons we wanted to go North. Some were common and others were not. One man had troubles at home, and he wanted to get as far away from his problems as possible. But for many of the men, this was the first opportunity in their lives to earn good money. As with many involved in World War II, all of the men had something of a patriotic feeling as well. I had my own reasons. Mainly, I had found a way to follow my dream of getting to Alaska. The Inside Passage was smooth sailing. For about twenty miles, the vessel was exposed to the Pacific Ocean, and the ship pitched about like a thimble atop the waves. When the vessel stopped in Ketchikan to fuel, we all stayed on the ship. From a distance, we spotted a glacier near Juneau, and the captain went off course specifically to show us a wrecked ship that had stuck the rocks years earlier.

After five glorious days of enjoying the Alician, the ship pulled into port at Skagway, Alaska, the northernmost port on the Inside Passage. I stood on the deck and studied the majestic mountains providing a dramatic backdrop for Skagway. Intoxicated by beauty greater than I'd ever imagined, I was anxious to set foot on Alaskan soil. Savineimi blood rushed through my veins. My adventure was truly beginning.

1942 Chugging Up The White Pass

After five days aboard ship, I'd grown sea-legs. I walked off the gangplank oceanographer for the sudden stillness beneath my feet. Having grown accustomed to the gentle movement of the sea, my first steps on Alaska soil felt peculiar. It would take awhile to adjust and get my land-legs back. I discussed the unfamiliar sensation with a few of the guys while we waited for further instruction. The group milled around the pier, uncertain of what to do next.

We were instructed to carry our luggage to an old empty store on the Main Street of Skagway, just a short walk from the pier. You would have thought I would have learned something about traveling light after my experience of going to Cody with Alfred. Unfortunately, I hadn't thought that far ahead, forgetting exactly how my footlocker would get from one place to another. Then again, there wasn't anything in it that I wanted to leave behind. There were insignificant belongings, but they were all mine. I walked slowly, lugging the footlocker, towards Main Street, fascinated by my new surroundings and temporarily forgetting the heavy weight.

Skagway was just like the frontier town that I had imagined it to be. The boardwalk was an interesting mixture of hotels, stores, and saloons. I imagined prospectors assembling their gear during the Klondike Gold Rush, getting ready to climb the treacherous mountain terrain and cross raging rivers in search of fortune. I was ecstatic to walk the same ground that outlaw "Soapy" Smith and good guy Frank Reid had walked on then. A narrow-gauge train traveled down the middle of Main Street, giving it an unusual charm.

I saw some of the guys I'd arrived with going into a building. I hurried in that direction. I was relieved to finally set the heavy footlocker down. I realized that there wasn't any place to sit except on our luggage. My footlocker was particularly comfortable, the only advantage that I'd discovered so far. We visited, anxious for the train to Whitehorse to depart. A few of us picked out a train car to ride in and built a fire in the stove so that it would be plenty warm by departure time for Whitehorse. When the whistle blew, the car was very toasty.

The two-engine train glided easily out of Skagway, but labored in the rough terrain of the White Pass. Movement was slow and difficult. The engine huffed and puffed, struggling forward. The mountain terrain, breathtaking to view, was an intense challenge for rail travel. The train twisted and turned, occasionally stopping to build up the steam necessary to repeat the performance.

I gazed at the jagged landscape, daydreaming about men who had gone before me. Strong determined individuals had climbed these same mountains years earlier using pack horses to carry supplies. One trip would have been hard enough, but many of the men made several trips to haul the supplies required by the Canadian Government. Now, I was a "Cheechako" in Yukon Territory, just a novice who didn't know the ways of the land and its people, and I was anxious to know how I would fare. Looking down on the untouched valley below, I realized that I had already discovered one of Alaska's many treasures.

The train came to a screeching halt at Lake Bennett. This was our chance to stretch our legs and eat. It felt great to walk around. The meal was served family style, and the excellent food was plentiful, reminding me of the huge feasts served to the threshing crews during harvest time in Minnesota. About an hour later, we boarded the train and continued to our final destination.

Arriving in Whitehorse, a frontier town on the bank of the Yukon River, I saw the town was alive with activity. It was immediately apparent that there were two distinct lifestyles here in the Northern Outpost, summer and winter. Posted on the wall of the train depot was a departure notice—THE FIRST RIVER STEAMER WILL DEPART SOMETIME IN MAY.

A detachment of Army personnel, civilian contractors, and all of their equipment had enlivened Whitehorse. Shacks and tents sprouted up amid the community of Caucasians, Indians, and many dogs. From the train, we were escorted to our quarters. E.W. Elliott Company had constructed a frame building for the cook's house. Fourteen white canvas tents stood neatly erected for the rest of the crew. Each tent had a wood deck inside with a wood stove.

At the campsite, my job was a fire tender for the fourteen tents. I was supposed to keep the tents warm for the crew by making sure the fires in the stoves were always burning. It was too soft a job for a young man. I had never gotten paid for such easy work.

The company issued eiderdown sleeping bags. Most of the guys wanted me to let the fires go out at bedtime and start them again about five a.m. I didn't even have to collect the wood for the stoves because that assignment was given to a day man who piled the wood carefully by each tent. There wasn't actually much work for me to do.

Before long, I discovered the baker was baking bread, rolls, cookies, and other goodies in the cook's house. I'd visit him, have coffee and eat some of his fresh bakery treats. Sometimes, I'd get sleepy and stretch out on the bench for a short nap between rounds of checking my fires.

Occasionally the baker would rouse me and say, "You'd better check your fires, kid." He wanted to make sure that I was doing my job.

In the morning, when my shift was over, I couldn't sleep. Light filtered through the white canvas tents, and noise from the equipment and scurry of people in and out of the tents kept me awake. I felt like I should be working during daylight hours, like about everybody else. One morning, on an impulse, I reported to the carpenter foreman. He put me to work, not knowing that I'd reported to him on my own. I filled out a time slip, just like the rest of the guys. It worked great until the timekeeper came across my name on two jobs.

"What the hell is going on here?" he exploded. "We can only pay you for one job!" I didn't get paid for the carpenter work. I didn't care. Although I hadn't seen a paycheck, I knew how much I should be getting, and it was more money than I'd ever seen in my life.

This fire tending job wasn't very exciting. I'd come all the way to Alaska to work on the highway project, and I wanted to be in on the action. I knew that I was the youngest guy around, but I was confident that I could handle a more complicated job, if they'd just give me a chance. I kept bugging my boss to get me a truck driving job. I reminded him that I'd driven a BIG beer truck in the Twin Cities, and that I had plenty of experience (just a slight exaggeration).

I knew that truck drivers got to be in the thick of things. I couldn't think of anywhere better to see everything from than behind the wheel of a big truck. I kept working on my foreman, dropping hints about truck driving. One morning, the foreman came to my tent just as I was getting off shift, with the magic words. "Roller-up, Kid. I've got a truck for you!"

Whoopee! Then, I panicked. The weather was getting much colder, and I didn't have any warm clothing, or, for that matter, any money because my first paycheck hadn't arrived. I remembered that my friend, Swede, had said, "If anyone in this tent needs money, I have a hundred dollars." Swede wasn't worried about anybody borrowing because he knew they would always pay him back. He was a fine man, but he was also a BIG man, six foot two and built like Paul Bunyan. His honest eyes demanded respect. I quickly found Swede to tell him about my truck driving opportunity, and the fact that I didn't have any warm clothes.

When I told him the news, Swede whipped out sixty bucks. "Here, Irv. If it's not enough, I'll give you some more," he said. I knew that I could count on him, and he didn't let me down.

"Thanks, Swede. I won't forget this, ever," I said gratefully. I rushed to the local store. The sixty bucks went a long way. I bought a wool mackinaw, wool socks, wool underwear, mitts, and felt boots (like a thick sock but nothing to go over them). All I needed now was a winter hat or cap of some kind. The store had only one cap left. It was wool, Canadian style. The only thing wrong with it was the size. It was 7 3/8 and I need 6 7/8. It was a might big but it had to do.

I was ready to see if I really was a truck driver. The foreman searched me out to show me my late 1930's model 3 yard G.M.C. truck. It was surplus from the Civilian Conservation Corp. It had been recently overhauled, and it looked nice. The only problem was that the heater wasn't working. It was a good thing that I'd been able to buy the wool clothing because I'd need it.

There were four of us to drive the trucks to the camp: the foreman, myself, and two other guys. A timber-cruiser was assigned as a passenger to ride with me. The trucks were loaded with as many barrels of diesel fuel and gasoline as they would hold.

I hadn't driven a dump truck before, and I wasn't sure how to dump the load. Before we went over to load the fuel, I experimented with the levers to see if I could dump it. I didn't have the nerve to ask anyone because I had told everyone that I was a truck driver. It didn't take me long to discover the combination to make the truck dump.

Before we left to head North the following morning, I said good-bye to my tent partners and Swede. He had become my closest friend in camp, although we hadn't known each other long. I promised him I'd send the money that I had borrowed as soon as I received my first paycheck.

Driving truck wasn't as hard as I feared. The rutted and soft areas of the trail were well frozen and the creeks were low. Of course, we couldn't travel fast. We took it easy, dropping our trucks into lower gear when necessary. The "Alcan" highway, as it became known, followed the general direction of an old established trail that went to the trading posts north of Whitehorse.

We arrived at Mrs. MacIntosh's Roadhouse around midnight. E.W. Elliott Company had arranged for her to feed the men whenever they arrived, regardless of the hour. After Mrs. MacIntosh's husband died, she continued running the trading post. She was a spunky old lady to continue running this type of business on her own. Before the foreman woke up Mrs. MacIntosh, he gave us a briefing. He knew very well that men living in camps without the presence of women had a tendency to get somewhat rowdy and slip their manners.

"Don't forget there is a lady present," he warned, "If you have to take a leak, go in the woods."

After the warning everyone treated Mrs. MacIntosh with respect and their best manners. We were thankful for her good meals and her kindness.

After breakfast, we checked our oil and pumped fuel into our tanks from the barrels that we were hauling north. The next day was smooth as we continued to take it easy according to the conditions. There weren't bridges on the creeks or rivers, so crossing them caused our brakes to freeze. The rivers were as low as they would ever get. Rivers like the Duke and Dutchess and the Donjek were divided into several different channels, so we could pick our way across.

On the second day, we arrived at Burwash Landing at 6:00 p.m. The trading post owner, Jean Jacquot, was a Frenchman who was warm and cordial, and he quickly invited us to supper. His niece Babe, a French Indian girl, served us a meal of moose meat, a first for me, with all the trimmings. Her silky black hair and slender figure brushed my shoulder as she set the large platters on the table. I longed to say something to her, but I was too shy. Babe was quiet, not speaking to anyone, but I did notice her watching me a few times with expressive brown eyes.

After the meal, the foreman went to his truck and returned with a bottle of whiskey. He had a whole case of whiskey in his truck, which was against all of the rules. He passed the bottle around for everyone to take a swig and then Jean and the foreman sat down alone to visit.

The rest of us guys were just getting comfortable when the foreman came over to tell us to fuel the trucks, check our oil, and head for Edith Creek. DRAT! Jean's niece only had half the table cleared. She was so lovely to watch, her movements so graceful.

As I walked out the door, I took one last look back at Babe. I'd just discovered a second Yukon treasure, and someday I'd come back to see her again.

BIG CAP TRUCK DRIVER (1942)

1942 Driving Truck in Edith Creek

We arrived at the camp around midnight. On the right-hand side of the road going North, just a few miles south of Edith Creek, several lanterns glowed through white canvas tents, penetrating the darkness. The noisy trucks signaled our arrival, and the foreman who was second in command hurried out to greet us and make tent assignments.

I pulled my truck up as close to my tent as I could get it. By now, most everyone had been roused from their sleep. The three men that I would share the tent with were in their mid-to-late thirties, older than me, and certainly old enough to be in the Army if they chose to be. I hauled my belongings into the tent as quickly as I could and settled down on my cot so everyone could get back to sleep. Laying in the dark with my new tent companions, I was just beginning to relax when a whisper came out of the blackness, the message crisp and clear.

"If that guy with the big cap is a truck driver, then I'm an aviator!" I cringed. There wasn't any questioning who the critic was talking about. After that comment, all I could think about was how I'd show these guys that I was as good a truck driver as anybody else. Out of sheer exhaustion, I gradually slipped into a sound sleep.

In the morning, I wasn't sure what to do so I hung around the truck waiting for further instructions. One of the men I was bunking with came over to the truck and started snooping around. He checked the truck over and started it up. I was beginning to get nervous, sure that he was trying to get the truck away from me, when the foreman came over.

"Is this the truck you drove up?" the foreman asked.

"Yes. Yes, it is," I quickly replied.

"Go back to the truck you've been driving," the foreman told my bunk companion. "This truck is his," he said, pointing to me. I was very relieved to hear the foreman say that because I was getting well acquainted with the truck, and I didn't want to switch to another one.

The camp was modest, consisting of several 12' x 16' wood-framed white canvas tents that had wood decks inside. One large tent included picnic tables with the benches firmly attached. The bullcook kept the fires burning in the tents and supplied wood by each tent. He also kept a barrel of water heating on a campfire. Each tent had four cots and a small table for a wash basin and water bucket. When the crew returned from work, the first man into the tent would fill the bucket with hot water from the barrel and bring it to the tent. There weren't any bathing or laundry facilities other than the wash basin. I was too shy to wash very thoroughly with the other guys in the tent, so I tried to do it when nobody was there.

There were about twenty men in the camp, including the camp foreman, gravel foreman, cook, bullcook, mechanic, grease monkey, shovel man, grader man, and Bureau of Public Roads timekeeper. There were also two wood-cutters and nine truck drivers. Everybody put in twelve hour days, seven days a week. I never went into the mess tent after we finished eating. I knew some card playing and drinking went on in there later in the evenings.

As the weather got colder, and conditions got tougher, our foreman and two or three of his good friends got snookered up. They must have been drinking all night. At breakfast, the foreman stood up in the middle of his table and challenged anyone to fight him.

He started singing loudly, "I am safe in the arms of Jesus, you! By Jesus Christ I am, I am Jesus' little man." As the foreman sang, providing gestures and movements to accompany the little tune, two men stood silently watching the show at the flap of the big tent. Mr. E.W Elliot and the headman of the Bureau of Public Roads (BPR) weren't impressed. They didn't say a word, and they didn't have to. The look on their faces said it all. The two men turned and left. That was the beginning of the shake-up in the chain of command. The BPR man wanted to fire the foreman immediately. But Mr. Elliott was a bit kinder and convinced the BPR man to demote the foreman to dumpmaster. The dump master was then promoted to foreman.

A daily routine soon became established at the camp. After breakfast, we got into a closed truck that the men called the "Paddy Wagon" so that we could be transported to our work site. When we arrived at the creek, where the gravel pit was, we checked out our trucks and started hauling gravel. We crossed the creek, actually driving in the creek for several yards to make it to the other side. Our brakes were frozen much of the time, and unusual ice cones would quickly build up on each wheel.

The gravel foreman kept a fire going with a large bucket of coffee constantly heating to warm us up. The trucks without heaters were really cold. The drivers of those trucks had to put a big rock on the fire to heat, exchanging it on every return trip. It helped—I put my feet on the warmed rock with my felt boots and it felt good. The bullcook came to the site everyday at noon, driving a dump truck and delivering a large kettle of stew. The food always tasted great.

Everyone worked hard. We became very filthy by day's end, especially the grease monkey. His clothes reeked of diesel fuel and grease, and he had an almost constant cough. The mechanic had a rough job trying to keep everything working. He had a small white canvas tent to keep his tools in and all his work had to be done outside. Most of the parts that he needed weren't available and the mechanic "made-do." A few trucks had their wheels welded directly onto the drums because the wheel lugs had broken off. Day after day, the routine continued. I began to get worried. I hadn't received a paycheck yet. I wanted to pay Swede back as soon as possible. I tracked my boss down and explained my situation. He told me that a truck was going to Whitehorse, and I might meet the paymaster at Burwash Landing. My boss granted me permission to make the trip.

I was lucky, and the paymaster was at Burwash Landing when we arrived. I received my first pay in cash. I gave $60.00 to the paymaster and asked him to give it to Swede. I then had $60.00 left. I bought some more warm clothing, including a wool sweater, a flannel shirt, and some socks. I had $1.00 left. "What can I get for one dollar?" I asked Jean, the trader.

He took a beautiful pair of moose skin baby slippers off the shelf. "How about these?" They were so cute I couldn't pass them up, and so I spent my last buck.

The guys back at camp had teased me about wanting to go to Burwash Landing to see that pretty French Indian girl. Of course, it crossed my mind many times, and I had hoped that it would happen. But it didn't. I cranked my head everywhere trying to see if Babe was around. She wasn't in sight, and I didn't have the nerve to ask Jean about her.

After I returned to camp, the weather started getting colder. Often, it was thirty degrees below zero or colder. The truck drivers didn't shut the trucks off in the severe weather, except to check the oil. It was too time consuming for the drivers to start cold trucks every morning, and the vehicles weren't winterized for cold weather. We ran out of anti-freeze for the radiators on some trucks, and the next best thing was diesel fuel. The dump beds on the trucks were left up at night so the oil would loosen up a little when the dump beds were let down in the morning.

I had my share of trials and tribulations in camp, mostly pranks saved for greenhorns. An old timer sent me for a tool that was nonexistent. When I asked a driver if he knew what it was, he sent me to another driver. After the third driver, I caught on that they were having fun at my expense.

The guys in my tent were always trying to outdo one another in the number of loads of gravel that they hauled. I thought the way to do it was to go as fast as you could with every load. I passed an old timer slowly chugging along. He let me know in no uncertain terms to stay behind him, no matter how slowly he was going! I learned the easiest and quickest way to back up to the shovel, and things went better as time went on. The original three guys I bunked with had either quit or got fired, so I figured I was doing better than they had.

Our shovel man had worked the shovel for a long 150 miles or more, and it was cold and miserable for him. Like most shovels at the time, the cab was open and very little heat came from the engine.

There were 3 Mack twelve-yard chain drive rock hauling trucks, and several GMC three-yard trucks like Fords and Chevys. I had a three-yard GMC. An old timer in his seventies drove one of the most difficult trucks, a four or five-yard Brockway. There wasn't a rear window or cab guard and not much for floor boards. Every time they loaded his truck, gravel spilled into the cab, and the old timer would have to scrape it out. The linkage was missing from his dump levers, so he had to crawl under the truck every time he dumped to let the dump bed down.

The weather got so cold that often the truck beds refused to come down at all. As it became more and more difficult to complete work, word started circulating that the project was winding up, and that we might break camp and head for Whitehorse.

On a bitter cold November evening in 1942, the first convoy of 6x6 Fairbanks freight trucks came through our camp. Everyone watched with interest as the procession of heavily loaded, noisy, large trucks passed by. Each truck had a large sign on the front end that read "FAIRBANKS FREIGHT." Now those are big trucks, I thought to myself. I didn't know that I would become intimately acquainted with the Fairbanks freight trucks, and not from the driver's seat.

The severe weather continued until work at the camp came to a complete halt. Everyone stayed in camp, just trying to stay warm as the still cold air penetrated our tents. The only sign and sound of life were the woodcutters doing their best to keep up the wood supply, which had dwindled down to almost nothing. The men had the stoves fired up hard because it was brutal cold and they were in tent all day. The woodcutters hauled wood from a burn not too far away, but it was impossible to keep up. They chopped or hand-sawed the trees, loading them in the dump truck, and then sawing them into stove-sized length for the tents.

I volunteered to work with the wood crew. Loading some of the heavier fire-killed logs was exhausting. I didn't think I'd last out some days. We all looked rough. The black charcoal from the fire-killed trees rubbed off on our clothes. My hair was getting long and so was my scraggly beard.

1942 On To Whitehorse

Finally, after four or five days of waiting, we got word to close down the camp. The foreman announced that the next morning after breakfast, each group would disassemble their tent, frame and stove and load it into a dump truck. When the pieces were all loaded, all hands would help to take down the big cook tent, and then we would all head for Whitehorse.

There were seventeen trucks all under their own power except one truck being towed. There was a yard full of trucks at camp that were broken down, but they were left to be tended to in the spring.

It was a slow trek to Whitehorse. The road was glaciered badly with ice and water. We often left the road and traveled on the lake. The lead truck tried to locate a place where we could climb out off the ice and get back onto the road. Unable to find a suitable spot, our procession stayed on the lake until an Army 6x6 came in sight. It was the first vehicle we had seen other than our own. There weren't any Army camps or Civilian Construction Camps on the stretch of road, except for the Powell Construction Company where we had stayed the previous night. The Army truck pulled or winched all the trucks back onto the highway where we belonged.

The trip tested every truck driving device I had learned and drew on strengths that I didn't know I had. Often I wondered if we would ever make it back. But after the Army truck got us off the lake, the convoy continued to move slowly forward. Late that evening, we finally arrived at Whitehorse.

Elliott's Camp was quite a surprise now. Changes had been rapid and significant, just like in all of Whitehorse. Now the camp even had a wash house, and it was one of the first places that I went. What a luxury! I soaked in the hot water and felt like I was in another world. It was the first bath I had taken since leaving Seattle, and it felt fabulous. I closed my eyes and reflected on the arduous journey from Edith Creek to Whitehorse. The guy with the big cap really was a truck driver, wondering how the "aviator" who didn't last was doing.

1942 *Freezing in Freight Trucks South*

The Highway wasn't completed, but there wasn't much more work that could be done until spring. Company rules called for employees to be returned to their place of hire. All the men, after they were paid, were supposed to go back to Seattle or Minneapolis, or wherever they hired on.

I had a problem. There was nothing for me to do in Seattle where I had hired on. I didn't have a home in Minneapolis anymore. My parents were relocating. My dad was already working in Fort St. John, British Columbia, and my mother planned to move as soon as she sold the house. I didn't know that Pa had hired on the Alaska Highway project in Minneapolis not long after I had hired on in Seattle. I asked at the office if I could be terminated in Whitehorse. I must have been talking to the right person because I convinced him to release me in Whitehorse. I still had some planning to do, but that was the first step. All I had to do was figure out a way to get to Fort St. John.

Someone told me to go see the Army lieutenant in charge of the Fairbanks freight trucks, which the Army used. The trucks traveled north with loads and south empty. I located Lieutenant Love with little difficulty. The lieutenant listened sympathetically. His eyes were gentle and kind. When I finished, he said, "Well, son, I don't see any reason why you can't ride the empty Fairbanks freight trucks going south. Wait here a few minutes. I'll be right back."

Soon, Lieutenant Love returned with a piece of paper in his hand. "If anyone gives you any trouble, show them this," he said, handing me a typewritten letter granting me permission to travel the Alcan Highway south to Fort St. John via empty Fairbanks freight trucks. That letter became my passport to get home. I didn't have any idea where I would stay, or for that matter what I would eat, but I decided to take my chances and make do with whatever was available.

Lieutenant Love told me where to go to find the trucks heading south and wished me a good trip.

I soon located an empty truck.

"Can I have a ride South?" I asked the driver.

"Sure," he replied, "but you'll have to ride in the back. There's three of us in the cab already."

I didn't have a very good traveling outfit. I had my sleeping bag and a footlocker of stuff that I didn't need. The weather was at least thirty degrees below zero, and I soon realized that it was going to be a very cold trip. The steel deck in the back of the truck felt like a solid block of ice.

The truck headed down the trail, abruptly stopping near Marsh Lake to pick up a young Canadian man. He had worked at a mine in the area and had planned to walk to work in Vancouver. He was a little better prepared than I was, but he lacked the warm clothing that this trip would require. His moccasins weren't large enough for several pairs of socks and his feet quickly started to freeze. I let him put his feet between my legs to try to keep his feet warm. We both did the same with our hands. Later I gave him an extra pair of socks that I had, and we both crawled into our sleeping bags.

The truck stopped for the first time at a small Army installation. The soldiers got out and went into a small frame building. The young man and I presumed that it was a mess hall. We decided to go in and see if we could eat too, and we were both grateful when they said, "Sure, why not?"

From that point on, our accommodations were a bit more challenging. The first night we built a fire and cooked some grub that the Canadian had. We sat by the fire, but we couldn't sleep all night because it was so cold. Stopping at another camp, we noticed a line forming outside a tent. Each soldier had a mess kit so we presumed it was a chow line. The tent opened on the side to serve the food. The Canadian and I didn't have a mess kit but we stood in line anyway. The food server put a hunk of meat and a piece of potato on a thick slice of frozen bread for us. The soldiers took their food to their tents to eat. We just stood outside and ate ours.

Each Army camp consisted mainly of tents. The camp we stopped at one night had just assembled a Quonset hut for the men to sleep in. It was so crowded that there was only about eight to ten inches between the cots. We wanted to sleep in the Quonset hut too and asked if we could.

"If you can squeeze yourselves between the cots, I guess it would be okay," a soldier replied. I was so tired that I quickly wedged myself between two cots and fell asleep. Sometime later, a soldier who had been playing cards by the stove felt his way in the darkness. He stepped on me.

"What the hell is down there?" he hollered.

"I'm here," I yelled back. "And I have permission to stay for the night," I quickly added. Anything was better than sleeping outdoors. The temperature now well below forty degrees below zero.

Another time we stopped at a civilian camp for lunch. Everyone was welcome to eat regardless of whom you worked for or who you were. Meal sheets were posted for sign up. A place on the form asked who you worked for, Army or civilian, and a badge number if you had one.

"What should we put down?" my Canadian friend asked.

"I'm going to put my Elliott number down," I replied. "Why don't you just make up a number?" And that's exactly what he did.

At Teslin Lake, the driver stopped to talk to a guard for instructions. It didn't sound like there was any danger crossing the ice with an empty truck, but he was instructed to hold the doors open while crossing the ice, just in case. Rumor had it that a truck did go through the ice.

We finally got to Watson Lake, and I had lost track of the days. I didn't even realize that the truck had gone several miles off the highway, and that's where he had left us. An airfield was under construction. I was getting more proficient at traveling with the footlocker. If I had very far to walk, I tied a line on it and dragged it behind me like a sled. There were many new frame buildings, some for an Army detachment and some for civilians, at the construction site. My Canadian friend and I weren't sure what the project was all about. We went over to the civilian camp and started asking a few questions and soon discovered that this was a Canadian contractor. We asked about getting a job. The foreman said he could hire the Canadian lad but not me.

It was well past working hours. The foreman directed us to a place where we could find a bunk and get some supper. We both slept great. In the morning we had a good breakfast and departed. My Canadian friend didn't want to work if I couldn't work too. We had become a traveling team.

We decided to investigate how we could again connect with a 6x6 freight truck heading South. We didn't find one that day, and again we were faced with the problem of where to stay for the night. We were wandering around trying to keep warm, when a Mountie tapped me on the shoulder and directed us to his office. He said he had a few questions to ask us.

"Who are you connected with?" the Mountie asked.

"Nobody," we replied in unison. I suspected that the contractor had reported us because we took after off after some good sleep and a couple of meals. The Mountie asked the Canadian a few questions. Then he started in on me. I showed him my credentials, my release papers from my job in Canada, and my permission to travel south on the Fairbanks freight trucks. He wasn't impressed.

"You damn Americans think you own this country," he said sarcastically. "Get your butt out of my sight and stay out of it!"

I didn't know what was bugging him, but I wasn't going to stick around to find out. We were doing our best to get out of there. We checked every truck we saw coming or going to see if it was leaving for the highway. With no luck finding a truck heading south, we looked for a place to eat and sleep, away from the domain of the mean-spirited Mountie. We knew better than to go back to the Canadian contractor. Surely, we were not welcome there.

We headed for the Army installation to see if we could eat with them. That wasn't a problem. We then located a small building that was a boiler room. We curled up for the night.

The next day we found a truck going back to the highway, where we would have a chance at finding another truck going south. We rode several freight trucks all the way to Fort St. John. Then it was time to say goodbye to my Canadian friend. He'd been a great traveling companion, and I wondered how long it would take him to reach Vancouver.

It had only been twelve days since I left Edith Creek. Suddenly, I was very anxious to see Pa. I thought back to all the urging I'd done to get him to come north to Alaska. Now on his own terms, here he was. Like father, like son.

1942 Fort St. John at Last

"You've changed, Irvin," Pa said pleasantly, happy to see me again. He was right. I had changed. Physically, I looked very rugged, especially after not having a haircut or shave for four months. And I finally did get my neck clean, but I'd changed inside, and I knew that was what Pa really meant. Irvin was maturing. It was inevitable.

"What are your plans now, Irvin?" Pa asked.

"I'm going to look for a job," I replied confidently.

"Good, Irvin, good," Pa said cheerfully. With a little experience under my belt, I now knew the correct answer to this loaded parental question.

But it wasn't easy to find a place to stay in Fort St. John. Unless you were working for a company or were in the Army, accommodations were hard to come by. I couldn't stay with Pa. All he had was a cot at quarters provided by the Oaks Construction Company. Pa worked nights so, at first, I slept in his cot while he was working.

The hardy homesteaders in Fort St. John, a frontier town forty miles north of Dawson Creek and the railroad, were having tough times. There wasn't enough demand for products produced locally. Most of the homesteaders lived a humble life, but they had good spirit and the ability to find humor under difficult circumstances, two ingredients that helped carry them through the rough times. It wasn't until a few construction families moved into the area that the local economy finally started to improve. Fresh eggs and milk were among the few commodities that were always needed.

I checked with E.W. Elliott Company about getting a job, and soon, I was again gainfully employed. Pa had made arrangements to rent a small cabin because Ma had sold the house and was due to arrive any day. I was glad to be working again and to have a steady place to stay.

Part of my job at E.W. Elliott consisted of bringing the cook's laundry to a local family for washing. That was how I met Katherine, Pearl, and Laura Mutter. I never dreamed delivering laundry could be so much fun. The spirited, giggly Mutter girls were the highlight of my work days in Fort St. John. Lively chatter and gentle teasing welcomed me on every visit. These young women found joy and fun in everything, including their work, which wasn't nearly as entertaining as they were.

Soon after my mother arrived, I started to get itchy feet again. My folks were just beginning to raise mink and Nutria, a South American Beaver. My dad's plan was when we were established a little better we would move to Grand Rapids and raise our animals. Pa said, "If we have a hundred dollars clear in the fall, we will make it." The war upset our lives, leaving us wondering what was in store.

My eighteenth birthday was approaching. That meant I could go to Minnesota and sign up for the draft. I was finally old enough to go in the service, and that prospect seemed a whole lot more exciting than the work I was doing at the time for E.W. Elliott Company.

NAVY (1942-1946)

Off to War

It was time for me to leave Dawson Creek BC Canada and travel by train to Minnesota to sign up for the draft. The first thing I did was look up my dear friends, the Pearson family. They were home and greeted me like one of their own. I explained why I came down and the response was, "You're just in time. We're right in the middle of mink breeding season."

In about ten days the draft board lady called.

"Are you ready to go?"

"Yes, Ma'am," I said.

"That's fine. Report to Ft. Snelling at 10:00 a.m. tomorrow morning."

"Yes, Ma'am. I will be there."

I reported in with about 200 other guys. We were directed to a large auditorium for our first instructions. "Do you see those empty coffee cans next to your aisle? They are butt buckets, understand? Use them. Is there anyone present that's interested in being a paratrooper?"

No one spoke up.

"If there are no more questions, wander down the lane and you will see 5 small chow halls. Pick one out and you will be served some very good food."

It was close to the end of the month. Their quotas were almost full. They needed 1 marine, 7 sailors and the rest, army. I got in the Navy line. The officer stamped "Approved for Navy."

Don Pearson drove me to the train depot to board the train. Most of the young men had girl friends or family members to send them off to the unknown. I have to admit I was lonesome without family. Thank God Don was with me.

It took awhile for people to find an empty seat and settle down. I waved to Don till he was out of sight. As the train moved slowly out of the city, memories flowed. There wasn't a flat wheel on this car. After listening to the train wheels clickty-clack, I finally fell asleep.

Farragut Training Station, Idaho

We arrived at Athol, Idaho about 3 a.m, and we all piled out. A couple of school-type-buses were waiting to haul us down to Farragut to the training station. One man was there to greet us and tell us to rest wherever we could, that someone would rouse us.

At 5 a.m. several people arrived. There were a few barbers, having a good time.

"Do you want to save your mustache?"

"Ja, sure."

"Well, hold your hand up under your nose to catch it, 'cause it's going to fall to the deck!"

A couple of guys issued clothing.

"Hey, this hat doesn't fit."

"It will have to do till we get one that does."

A couple of guys helped us ship our civilian clothing home. A bugle blasted away, playing "Doggy-doggy-doggy, come and get your bone."

The Master at Arms (MA) told us what line to get into for our first meal. He carried a Billy club and walked back and forth. After about 20 minutes, the MA told me to take my hands out of my pea coat pockets. "My hands are cold," I said. "I'm not taking them out." The MA jerked me out of line and put me on the end of the line. He pulled me out twice more till I was the last one in the mess hall. *Did I really volunteer for this dumb outfit?*

Next I had to guard the clothes line at midnight and not a stitch of clothing on the line. It took me some time to absorb what they were trying to teach me.

We were allowed three choices to pick the unit we were interested in. My three choices were all the Armed Guard. This duty was to protect merchant ships with a Navy gun crew. It wasn't long before I started to understand the principle of training kids off the streets or farms. Our government was desperate to get our troops out on the battle field. It was OK with me. We completed our six weeks of training and were sent to gunnery school.

Gunnery School, San Diego

The Chief Petty Officer who was in charge had an entirely different philosophy of how to train people. The large group of us listened with ears wide open so we didn't miss anything.

"We have a good Navy Base here, and I'm sure you will like it. We feed you well. Eat all you want, but be sure you eat it all. If you don't like something just put your hand above your food tray and you won't be served that particular item and they won't slop gravy on top of your pie either. When we have a short arm (penis) inspection shortly before you are served a meal, you are given time to wash your hands." This Chief Petty Officer was good to us green sailors. If he asked me to jump in the ocean, I would have.

We were trained to be familiar with the 5" 38 (built in Minneapolis), the 4", and 3" cannon and 20 mm anti-aircraft guns. We had to practice with all these weapons except the 5"51. That I would learn on the Gulfwax, my first ship. We practiced shooting at targets towed with aircraft, also a radio controlled small model plane about 12" long and rockets that we never hit. We trained in all positions, pointer (up and down), trainer (horizontal), and other duties on the 5"51 because there were more things to be familiar with.

The Tanker Gulfwax

My first ship, the Gulfwax, was an old tanker build in 1926, which retired from service before WWII. Its hull and deck plates were plenty rusty, although it looked seaworthy. This was my first experience on a sea-going ship, sailing with 21 Navy shipmates and a Merchant Marine crew. Our Navy crew consisted of 1 lieutenant, 1 radio man, 1 signal man, 1 Coxen and a 2 c gunners mate. The remaining men were all 1c seamen, including me.

One of our weapons was a 5"51 salvaged off an old battleship. Basically a broadside, it was not for aircraft unless flying very low. The 5"51 required a trainer, a pointer, three projectile loaders, three powder bag loaders, a rod man for the six foot pole to seat the projectile, a tray man to handle the funnel-type tool to put in the breach to avoid damaging the inner breach, and a gun captain to put a 30 caliber shell in the outside of the breach when the barrel was loaded. He also guessed the range and then pulled the lanyard to set off the powder bag, and opened the breach and pressed the air lever to blow out any sparks.

Crossing the Equator on the Gulfwax

If you haven't crossed the Equator you are a Pollywog. When you have crossed the Equator, you become a Shellback. When we crossed the Equator, four of us were on watch, so we had to wait till we were relieved for this important ceremony. Before hand, they stretched out a canvas tube about 35' long with steel hoops about 3' apart to keep the tube round, and about 3 feet in diameter. Its real purpose is to be hoisted full length over the hatch cover to allow the fumes to escape from the cargo hold. For this ceremony, it remained on the deck.

As a man went through, all the other sailors got on each side of the tube and beat on top of the canvas with a twisted wet towel. A 21'2" salt water hose shot water through the tube as the poor victim tried to crawl through faster than the water is getting in. When he did get to the outlet, two guys were waiting for him with paint brushes loaded with primer paint. They poked you in the face or any place else. I was the last one to go through, so there were about 20 guys working on me. I had to fight to get out of the tube. My hair, nose and ears were plastered with paint. I couldn't find anything but paint thinner to clean my ears, blow it out of my nose, and wash my hair. My skull was so dry my hair was just breaking off. That's what I blame for becoming a chrome dome.

Scary Stories

Two trips on the Gulfwax were very scary. The first trip was to New Caledonia, 1400 miles east of Australia, where the major city was Noumea. We didn't travel in convoy because when the flues were blown, the smoke would give our position away, even beyond the horizon, which you could see for about 30 miles distant.

There was only one dock on the east side of the Island of New Caledonia, and only one small building for the custodian. We were at the dock for three or four days pumping oil into storage tanks when a Destroyer Escort arrived to guide us away from the port. We hadn't traveled very far when our escort detected a submarine. The escort crew discharged several depth charges and made a strike, thanks to our savoir-faire. The escort stayed with us for another two or three hours and left us. We were on our own the 26 days it took to get all the way to San Luis Obispo, California.

Another scary experience with the Gulfwax was on a trip to Adak, Alaska. We ran into a terrible storm, even worse than the two typhoons I would be in in the South Pacific. When the tanker bow came out of the water, we breached like a whale when it slaps back in the water. The whole ship quivered and shook without support under its bow. When the stern came out of the water, exposing the propeller, it shivered and shook like a dog shaking a squirrel. I'm sure the captain and first mate left some brown spots on their underwear. Us green kids didn't have brains enough to realize this was no ordinary storm. We lost one life boat and the forward gun tub was damaged. To our relief, by the time we arrived at Adak the storm had subsided, so we put our 20 mm back in the gun tub to clean and lubricate. As we approached the harbor, the strangest and most unbelievable sight lay before our eyes. A Russian lend-lease Liberty Ship had broken in half just forward of its bridge and came into port under its own power. The bow was lying on its side closer to the beach.

We had our troubles, too. Oil leaked from five cracked plates, leaving a slick behind. I'm certain our ship would have broken in half if we hadn't had a riveted hull. The Liberty Ships were all welded. It would have been impossible to keep the Gulfwax afloat with thousands of gallons of oil a couple of feet thick floating in the water. We would all have perished.

Man Overboard, San Francisco Bay

When we pulled into Port San Pedro in San Francisco Bay, it was still daylight. The pilot boat headed for the beach with half the merchant crew aboard. The ballast was pumped out long before we pulled into port. All we needed was a berth to tie up. The deck hands were missing, probably already at the closest honky-tonk. We were playing Pinochle on the deck when the first mate yelled at us, "Would any of you gun crew guys mind giving me a hand? All my blankety-blank crew are on the beach except the quarter master and mates."

I had a friend we called "Chief" who was a Papago from Arizona. He and I volunteered to help. By that time, it was pitch black, except for the first mate's three-cell flash light. Chief stepped into the scupper trough and fell.

"Man Overboard!" I yelled.

The mate and I both threw in life rings and hopped into the whale boat and banged our oars together a few times before we organized ourselves. A ship heading out to sea heard the commotion and threw out a couple of life rings, too. It was so dark we weren't sure which way to go. After about 30 or 40 minutes we spotted a tug with a bright light shining into the water, so we headed for it.

One of the tug crew yelled, "Are you guys looking for something?"

The mate yelled back, "We lost a man overboard. Have you seen him?"

"Ja, sure, we found him. He's OK, just a little hide scraped off his gut."

We got Chief loaded in the whale boat and rowed towards where we thought the Gulfwax might be. When we found it, we spotted the

Captain leaning on the safety chain by the gangplank. The captain hailed us aboard and said, "Thank God you're OK. You two boys can sit in my private chair any time you wish. Thanks for making it back."

The Captain was good to me. He taught me a couple of handy knots that were useful. He let the two of us paint the bridge with the union steward's permission. The coxen said, "Let the boys paint. We'll never get done painting this rusty tub."

The Captain said to me, "Ray, if you are ever looking for a seaman's job after the war, look me up and I'll put you to work." Wow – what a compliment!

Joining the Army Transport Sea Witch

When we'd been at sea for six months or more and came to an American port, we were allowed to go on leave for ten days or so. I qualified, so I went home to visit my folks at Fort St John, Canada for about three days, and then reported back to Treasure Island, California, to be introduced to another ship.

My new ship was the Sea Witch, a C-2 Army transport. Ship's company included merchant seamen, Navy gun crew, and Army medics. We could handle 1,800 passengers. Our first trip we picked up troops from Port Hueneme, California, and sailed to New Guinea and followed the coast north of Finchaven.

Crossing the Equator on the Sea Witch

The ceremony crossing the Equator on the Sea Witch was much different than what took place on the Gulfwax. Eighteen thousand were too many people to go through the Solemn Mysteries of the Ancient Order of the Deep. The military figured out a system that was fair. Each platoon or squad would choose one person to represent them. Everyone had to go below deck while the Shellbacks and our Chaplain prepared for the great event.

The Armed Guard were to be the police to keep order and escort the "lucky" ones through the proceedings. Some on the ship were combat marines. There was also a small group of men classified as "Special Services." Those with us were professional entertainers. There was a band, a hypnotist, singers, and a professional harmonica player who had performed for President Roosevelt. Special Services became the Royal Staff of King Neptune, including The Royal Baby, Royal Executor, Royal Barber, Royal Doctor and the Armed Guard Police.

When everything was ready, permission was given for the troops to come topside. Everyone looked for a good place to watch. Some shimmied on the cargo booms that were secured horizontally perhaps eight or ten feet above the deck; every foot of the booms was occupied, in addition to every available space on deck.

There was a lot of noise from the audience. One guy sitting on the boom yelled someone's name, so King Neptune commanded the Armed Guard Police to get that man and bring him to the Royal Baby. No one yelled names after that.

The first "volunteer," stripped to his shorts and blindfolded, was introduced to the Royal Baby, a Special Services man who weighed about 350 pounds. The victim was doused with water and told to kiss the Royal Baby. The Baby had bent his arm to make a wedged elbow, which was smeared with canned pumpkin to look and feel like baby doo-doo. If the victim hesitated, the Royal Police give him a nudge in the right direction. The victim's shorts were wet. His face had gunk on it. What could be worse?

The Royal Executor. The wet and "lucky" guy was told to sit in a chair to rest a minute. He sits in the chair and nothing happens . . .

until they crank up the magneto. "Wow! Wow! Wow! Shut it off! Wow!" He looks like a mess. What could be worse than that?

The Royal Doctor.

"Are you feeling OK?"

"Yes, Sir."

"You don't look so good. Perhaps you need some medicine." It's a bucket of cold spaghetti doused with Tabasco sauce. He throws it up. What could be worse than that?

The Royal Barber's Chair. A hair cut? That can't be too bad. The Barber smeared a tonic – honey –all over his head. Then the Barber took huge scissors to cut big chunks of hair off here and there. When the haircut was done, the Barber gave the chair a little push backward onto a trap. The victim plunged into a canvas tank about 10 feet square and 5 feet deep. It feels like the ocean. Two big guys grabbed the victim and hoisted him up and down, up and down, up and down three times. They slid him face first down a canvas chute full of garbage. I get the willies just thinking about it.

In New Guinea and Australia

A few days before we arrived at New Guinea, three small Japanese landing craft landed on the beach not far from the Army camp, intending to attack the Americans and Aussies. They failed to pull off a surprise attack, and all the Japanese were killed. We tied up and there was room for only one ship in the midst of the jungle. There were Australian soldiers, American soldiers, and New Guinea natives living in grass huts. The passengers we picked up from New Guinea were terribly injured, bodily and some mentally.

From New Guinea we followed the coast side of the Great Barrier Reef for protection from submarines and sailed to Sydney, Australia, where we left our 1,800 injured passengers. This reef is several hundred miles long, and it has been estimated that several hundred ships have sunk there over the centuries. Our crew was given "junk" jewelry for the natives who wanted to barter for cigarettes or jewelry and while going under the famous bridge at Sydney, two outrigger canoes approached our ship.

Oh! I'd better not forget the nice girls. Wow, what fun.

On the Move

We departed from Australia with a load of wool and tallow and sailed to Pearl Harbor to unload the cargo and load the 2nd Marines. They bunked on the second lower deck. All the holds below them were loaded with ammunition of all sizes.

From Pearl Harbor we sailed to Enewetok, an atoll about 3000 miles as the crow flies from Pearl Harbor, considering the zig zag course we were following. When we approached the island, we could see the ships at anchor before we could see the land. There were no trees; I understood that all the trees were destroyed when the Americans bombarded the island to take possession of it. This location was valuable because it was a perfect place to make up a convoy. Dozens of ships could anchor there safely. There was only one narrow entrance and it was protected with a net to open and close to let ships in and out.

Our fresh water supply was getting low with 1800 passengers, so our Captain rationed the water to ten minutes three times a day at the scuttle butt, for the drinking fountain and shower. Our passengers had to wash with salt water soap.

After a few days waiting we finally got our orders to leave and join a convoy. We didn't know where it was going. The trip was uneventful, the sea was calm. Our passengers had only two meals a day. They were always hungry. The Armed Guard were used to slow traveling, standing our watch, doing our chores and playing Poker or Pinochle, so time flew by rapidly. When we approached the island of Saipan, we knew we were in the war zone. There was a variety of ships blasting away at the island, as well as rockets from Tinian, three miles away.

I believe Admiral King, from the Battleship California, was in charge of operations. There were many large ships like cruisers and destroyers helping the bombardment continue day and night before we arrived. The Colorado was struck by a gun emplacement on a small island named Rota on the opposite side of Saipan where the 2nd Marines were landing. The Colorado was struck in the bridge. I never heard how many were killed.

The shelling finally subsided and preparations were underway to deploy the troops. All orders and instructions commuted by voice from Admiral King to an officer aboard a speed boat who transferred the message to whoever needed the information. The first message from the Admiral was for our Captain, a merchant seaman, to move the Sea Witch closer to the beach. Our Captain refused to go that close for fear of drifting into the coral lined beach. The Captain of any ship is "God" when it comes to being responsible for his ship.

When our troops went ashore, they found out that all the Japanese were not killed from the ships' earlier bombardment. The Admiral sent word to our Captain that about 300 casualties occurred the first 30 minutes or so. We didn't see any Japanese planes. The Americans were flying around Saipan to keep the enemy planes from getting close to the troops invading.

When the Sea Witch was preparing to leave the beach area we attempted to hoist the anchor with the capstan, but it didn't budge. The anchor was locked in the coral reef. Our Captain was right about the coral but still got in trouble. There was only one thing to do – cut the anchor chain off with a cutting torch and go about 5 miles out to sea. The capstan was damaged trying to pull up the anchor.

Jumping Ship

I had already served about a year. My buddy and I schemed about how to have a little shore leave in Saipan. We planned to jump ship in order to search for war trophies, like flags, swords, or Japanese guns. We asked two shipmates to stand our watch for us in case we didn't make it back in time. We had observed the military crew unloading ammunition off the ship. We decided that if we climbed down on the safety cargo net and then waited until the loaded net was dropped into a "Duck," we'd be on our way to the beach.

There were 3 or 4 Ducks floating around waiting to be loaded. When it was their turn, they lined up under the cargo net so that the winch man could drop it into the Duck. That's when my friend and I jumped on top of the ammunition and rode it to the beach.

After the fact, I admit it wasn't the smartest thing to do. We didn't realize our ship would be several miles out to sea, whether they damaged the capstan or not. Not only that, we weren't the only ones ashore. Ten more shipmates showed up at the same place we were expecting to get back on our ship. We were told where we could find a cache of rations. The marine said, "Let me warn you guys. Don't try to steal them or you might get shot." We stayed on the beach all night in the rain trying to figure out how we were going to get back to our ship. In the morning, we noticed a small ship anchored a half a mile or so away. We talked it over and decided "Flags," our signal man from Minnesota, could attract that vessel with two white hats for his signal device. He got a response right away.

Flags: "Can you bring us to our ship?"

Vessel: "Yes. We can take you if you can get to our ship."

We scouted around to see what was available. We spotted an "Alligator," a vessel like a big tub that's propelled with about 3 inch Growsers on each track to tread you through the water. We asked a soldier if that vehicle was his.

"Yes. It's mine. What's your problem?"

We explained and he said, "I'll take you to that ship. You might get a little wet when we go through the big wave." We were already wet. We piled in. We had no trouble getting to our rescue ship. We climbed aboard and got in line for hot coffee. Wow! What a great treat.

When we arrived at the Sea Witch, there was a congregation top side, leaning over the rail to see these renegades who had jumped ship. The Jacob's Ladder was already thrown over the side. The Sea Witch would roll one way and you would be up to your waist in water. When it rolled the other way, you would be a couple of feet out of the water. With the small landing craft and the Sea Witch both bobbing up and down, it was difficult to jump for the ladder.

Our Chaplain took pictures, our officer glared at us, and a bunch of our shipmates wise-cracked, "Hey! Why didn't you guys stay on the beach? Ha! Ha!"

Our names was posted on the bulletin board in our mess hall. We reported for Captain's Mast at 8 bells (4 o'clock) with clean shirts and white hats. We all pleaded, "Guilty, Sir."

Our officer said, "Gentlemen, to be fair with your shipmates, I'm required to decide what kind of punishment should be dished out. While all twelve of you were gone, your shipmates had to stand your watches. All of you shall spend the next 3 days making up watches that you missed. Plus, I am curious as to the numbers on the ammunition boxes on the bottom forward hold." (Our Officer was a good and fair man that stripped down to his shorts and worked with us in that dark sweltering hole.) We all agreed it was a very lenient punishment.

The Sea Witch had a tug escort to Pearl Harbor where it was scheduled for repairs. We brought half of the survivors and a second ship brought the other half to Pearl Harbor.

On the Attack Navy Transport Typhoon

With nothing much for us to do, my best friend "Axel" Ringhoffer and I went to visit a ship that was tied close to ours. It was an Attack Navy Transport, the Typhoon. This ship was entirely different from anything I sailed on and it looked very interesting. This ship was equipped with everything needed to actually make an attack. Ship's company was about 150 Navy crew members, including 11 officers. The Navy crew had coxens to man the landing craft, winchmen to lower the landing craft in the water and men to operate the weaponry, and a multitude of other skills it took to manage this complex ship.

The Typhoon needed two men for replacements. We were asked if we were interested.

"Hey!" I said, "Axel, let's take it."

Axel said, "Not me. You can take it. I like it where I am."

Well, I have to admit I was dumb enough to take it. The officer in charge was tough and in good physical condition. He would challenge all of us, "If you don't like the way I'm running things, step forward and we'll have a little 'tussle.'"

A few weeks later at uniform inspection, my officer said, "Savela, what is that thing under your nose?"

"That's my mustache, Sir."

"Why the hell are you trying to cultivate that under your nose when it grows wild around your short arm?"

It was only a few weeks later when he was cultivating a mustache under his nose. When he was through talking to us, he said, "Are there any questions?" I had to bite my tongue to keep from saying what he told me. Now that was smart on my part, because he was the kind of guy that would have had me put in the brig if I wised off to him.

While we were in a port, we had a uniform inspection before going ashore. One of our mates who had been painting his gun tub dripped gray paint on his shoes and decided to paint them gray. Our officer saw those gray shoes, chewed him up and down and wouldn't allow him to go ashore. On top of that, he said, "As soon as we get to a home port, I'll have your butt in the brig." This kid was so scared he jumped ship. Our officer put pressure on the people that were on duty at the gangplank, but nobody would admit that they allowed him off the ship. The official report was that he climbed the ship's Hawser to the dock.

I don't think I was even given a position with a gun crew on the Typhoon. I must have been on the Typhoon when I arrived in San Francisco. My best friend Axel Ringhoffer was in the Armed Guard building sitting on the deck, polishing a garbage can.

"Axel, what the heck are you doing there?"

"Can't you see? I'm doing a darn good job, too."

Axel said he didn't wake up that morning at Reveille. The building was at least 250' x 150'. The bugler blew Reveille three times on each side of this huge building and then played a lively song over the loud speakers: "Mares eat oats and does eat oats and little lambs eat ivy." Then the MA rattled the steel cots with his night stick – and Axel still didn't wake up.

The Appleton Victory, Battle joined

Axel and I were lucky to be together again and be assigned to the same ship that was fitted out at Portland, Oregon. Our new ship was named the Appleton Victory. These new ships were to replace the Liberty Ships for peace time service. Their cruising speed was 22 knots versus 11 knots for the Liberty Ships. Our ship the Appleton had a companion Victory Ship that was completed at the same time, so we wound up working with their group loading supplies on both ships before we were bound for sea.

Axel and I had plenty of time when our Navy obligations were done. We got a job cleaning decks and bilges for ships that were in for repair. One of them was a Russian ship that hauled German prisoners to the States.

While we performed our duties, we met a Russian man stoking six boilers with coal, a tough job shoveling from the bunkers and then shoveling the coal into the boilers. This man showed us his muscles and pointed to us. "No muscle." Axel pointed to his own brain and said, "More brain," in German, which the stoker understood.

We loaded all the ammunition, life jackets, helmets, paint and anything else the Armed Guard is responsible for. Two or three days before heading out to sea, the Head Chef ordered fresh produce and fresh milk. Seamen don't see fresh milk or vegetables for a long time. They are used to canned milk and canned veggies.

When all the last minute details were done, we headed down the Columbia River to enter the Pacific Ocean. The Victory ships didn't haul troops. They were strictly designed for hauling hardware and bulk loads of grain, etc., for peace time. We went someplace to load equipment such as Jeeps and bulldozers. They had to build a cat-walk above the load in order for the gun crew to get to our gun tubs.

Everything went smoothly till we entered a typhoon. It was risky with the high heavy load, but it was not nearly as bad as the North Pacific storm had been aboard the Gulfwax. We had to go past our destination of Okinawa and backtrack in a safer sea. Before we arrived at Okinawa we stood a full watch for three days.

Our officer held a meeting on the poop deck.

"Gentlemen, we are entering dangerous waters. Keep yourselves alert. Two regulars will stand their normal watch and the other four will stay in the gun tub day and night, and take turns eating. Wear your helmets and your life jackets."

We were on Red Alert for three days, expecting something to happen. Nothing did.

Our officer told us to go on regular watch the fourth day. We were told that a Japanese plane might follow one of our planes without lights on. Our planes would have their lights on to confirm that they were American. About 11 o'clock, a plane was flying very low, perhaps 30 feet above the water, when Sailor Stubby McGraw, who was on watch in the stern gun tub, called the Bridge to report, "It looks like a Jap plane approaching."

The first class gunner's mate yelled to our officer, "Should I turn on the alarm?"

Before our men got to our guns, the Cruiser about 40 or 50 yards from us fired at the plane and made a direct hit and blew it to smithereens. It was about 50 yards from our gun tub.

The next day when it started to get dusk, a small landing craft traveled slowly among all the ships in the harbor to dispense a form of fog that cloaks all the ships. It was odorless and you could hardly see the ship's bow from the Bridge.

The second night, a Japanese bomber dropped a string of bombs and struck a cache of gasoline barrels on the beach, which exploded and caused a huge fire. I don't know if anyone was hurt or killed in the explosion.

We wanted to shoot at the bomber with our largest cannon, the 5"38, but our officer said our 5" would not reach it. He was right. The Army was shooting at the plane with their 90 mm cannon and could not reach it. We could see their bursts falling short with the aid of three or four high powered lights shining on the plane. I would like to have seen one or two of our 5" shells set to 45 seconds and give the plane a long lead, but I don't know if our 5" had enough oomph to get up there.

When the fog lifted up, just 12 feet above the water was a Jap plane that attempted to dive into a Destroyer Escort. The trouble for the plane was he couldn't see the ship till he was almost on the water. The gun crew only had a couple of seconds to shoot the plane before the plane hit the ship. A direct hit blew the plane to Kingdom Come. We were within range but couldn't shoot at it because we would have been shooting at our own ship.

Our sister ship, the other new Victory we shared work parties with, was struck by a suicide bomber, carrying two 500 lb bombs. (After the war, research suggested this was not a bomber, but a Jake float plane.) The plane struck just forward of the Bridge. Our officer gave permission for our first class gunner's mate to visit our sister ship because we knew several of the boys on it. This ship may have been the only ship around the point of the main anchorage, a sitting duck for such a situation. I remember very vividly how our gunner's mate described the first loader that was struck by one of the cargo booms that fell on him and almost cut him in half. It shook me plenty, because that was my job.

Peace Time

After 30 some odd days, we headed back to Pearl Harbor for another load of cargo. We went back to Enewetak to be in a convoy again and return to Okinawa. Nothing exciting was happening. We were doing our routine chores, standing watch, replacing grease in our cannon barrels, painting the guntubs, etc. We must have been about half way between Enewetak and Saipan when our officer came around to each guntub and told us, "I think the war is over."

We were dumb-founded. We weren't even excited at first till it started to sink in.

"I'll be back and tell you when it's confirmed for sure, and then I want you to load and fire every round of ammunition in the ready boxes." That way, the Navy didn't have a problem of storing live ammunition. We all fired all our ammo. We had never had a chance to set our fuses at 45 seconds until now. Wow! What a long time it took for them to explode.

Our new lifestyle was beginning to take effect. Smokers could smoke day or night out on the open deck. We could leave the blackout curtains open at night to allow the fresh air in. Oh! What a glorious day it was!

One of our crew had enough points to be discharged. If I had been married, I would have had enough points, too. He was transferred to another ship going to the states. The rest of us were still going to Okinawa. Our ship would help prepare our country for peace again.

We stayed in Okinawa a month or more before our Captain received orders to sail to New York via the Panama Canal. I was offered to make that trip with one other person to remove all the Armed Guard equipment off the ship. I declined. A big mistake on my part I regretted ever since. Not really. I couldn't wait to get back to Alaska.

The Carrier Thetas Bay

The rest of us were scheduled to return to the States on the Carrier Thetas Bay. When my name was called on the muster list, I walked down to the beach in the rain with my duffel bag. We were instructed we could only make one trip; what you can't carry, leave it behind. Most of the sailors dropped their hammock off their sea bag, including me, because it was getting heavy because of the rain as we walked towards the Thetas Bay that was waiting for us. We had rain gear when we were aboard our ship, but not in our duffel that was with us.

After we got acquainted with the ship, we sat down on the deck and played pinochle. That was our first mistake. When the line had only a few people left, we got in line. The server said, "Sorry, mates, we are through serving." Later, they were short of scullery personnel. Doing this work allowed us to eat first and take a shower with fresh water. It was worth it.

The Thetas Bay arrived at the Navy base at Bremerton, Washington, when we were approached to sign up for another year. Only one sailor signed up.

Next we were transferred to Great Lakes Navy base and were encouraged again to sign up for another year. No takers from this group either.

1946 Discharged

I was discharged from the Navy at Great Lake Navy base in Chicago with my $300 mustering-out pay, early February 1946.

My Brother Bruce and the Navy

When we were children, our family moved so many times, my brother Bruce was set back twice, so Bruce and I were in the same grade.

Bruce finally got disgusted and ran away to Cody, Wyoming, where he worked setting up pins in a bowling alley owned by Buffalo Bill Cody's niece (and in a green house). Later he decided to join the US Civilian Conservation Corp (CCC) camp. A few months later he joined the Navy.

Bruce was a skilled artist and ivory carver. His choice for schooling in the Navy was pattern making. Bruce was in the Navy school for a year when World War II was declared. The Navy pulled Bruce out of pattern making and put him in the submarine repair section as a ship fitter. Bruce's submarine repair ship was stationed at remote islands for three years and five months, and his ship went to New Zealand once for a short time. Bruce said his ship got struck with a bomb or torpedo while he was in the tool room. The concussion blew him out of the tool room door. That's all he told me about it.

Bruce stayed in that trade till the war was over. He nearly completed his six year hitch. With just five more months to go, he was diagnosed schizophrenic and given a medical discharge. Bruce suffered all the rest of his life. He heard voices all the time, except when he was drunk. Sometimes he was picked up off the street and put in jail, with the police not knowing if he was drunk or out of medicine. My folks had Bruce put in an insane asylum, not knowing how hard it would be to get him released. Bruce finally outwitted the doctors by telling them the voices were gone over six months, although the voices were still there. This is what it took to get him out of the asylum. Bruce died when he fell down a flight of stairs and broke his neck.

UP THE ALASKA HIGHWAY

Alaska Was Calling Me

After I was discharged from the Navy, I rode in a passenger train (not on top of a box car, as I had done before) to Minneapolis and hitchhiked to Bloomington, Minnesota, from the Great Lakes.

I stayed in Bloomington for about three days. Alaska was calling me, so I climbed aboard another train headed north to Dawson Creek, British Columbia, the end of the rail and the "0" mile post for the Alaska Highway. To travel the Alaska Highway by auto or foot, I needed a permit, which I acquired from the Canadian Mounted Police.

I didn't have a vehicle – most of my money went for food. I bought a Duluth backpack at one of the remote Trading Posts in Canada and began to hitchhike the 1,522 miles to Fairbanks. There were so few vehicles that when I got one, I got a long ride. I stopped to visit my folks at Coal River Highway camp, not very far northwest of Liard Hot Springs, about a third of the way to Fairbanks. Gas and food were available about every one-hundred miles.

Border City

Border City, nearly 300 hundred miles from Fairbanks, was hatched by four men with visions to establish a city, perhaps a village, well, at least a trading post on their solid ground across the swamp from the Canadian Border. The first building constructed was made with locally cut logs. The floor was dirt. I'm quite certain it had a sod roof. It was dark inside. There was no question but that it was rustic. I bought a pair of Canadian socks there. Canadian socks were made large enough to slide over two pairs of socks without being too tight in mooseskin moccasins. American socks were longer, but were not wider, so they were too tight and wouldn't keep your feet from freezing.

The Future Delta Junction

When I got as far as the unnamed town now known as Delta Junction, the whole area was known as Big Delta. The village of Big Delta was eight miles north of the Junction, and it was located on a junction as well, a junction of rivers, not roads. There, the Delta River met the Tanana River.

John Hydukavich owned quite a large log building to put travelers up for the night, and a lady named Rika Wallen, who came from Sweden or Minnesota, cooked in the road house. Rika also had a house of her own and sold homemade bread. There also was a ferry that crossed the Tanana River and on the south side of the river there was a cabin for the ferry man. The Road Commission had a large shed for equipment and a small cabin for storage. There also was an abandoned Army Signal Corps log building in the same area. The Post office was pretty much a shack.

The place that would become Delta Junction was growing faster than Big Delta, with new people homesteading and entrepreneurs going into business. The Post Office from Big Delta was moved to Delta and the new town was named Delta Junction. (Years later I would serve Delta Junction for three years as the mayor.) I had $60 when I arrived in Fairbanks. I stayed in the Pioneer Hotel and I got a job at Cleary Hill Gold Mine the next day.

My Gold Mine

At the Cleary Hill Mine I was teamed with a middle-aged man, experienced working underground. I learned from him. I still had a lot to learn. Duane, with whom I would later mine, was the mill man.

Everything I suggested my partner didn't want to take the time to do, such as haul water from a spring a mile away. We needed it for drilling rock to keep us from breathing dust. I wanted to get advice for cribbing our shaft. I didn't want to gut the side of our shaft. He was a little crazy to get at the gold "right now." He took out $13,000 worth of gold gutting the sides after I sold out to him for $2000 plus what we had coming from the bank. It may have been a dumb thing on my part. I didn't trust my partner working underground. I had to think of something to justify my judgment.

A friend of mine, Mike Kupoff was the blacksmith at Cleary Hill Mine. Mike paid off a labor lien that was "hanging" for years to acquire the claim. He offered to pay what the original price was, but no accumulated interest. This claim was two and a half acres 10 feet off the Steese Highway (a narrow gravel road) about 18 miles from Fairbanks, and about 3 miles from Cleary Hill Mine. The big time mining company known as the FE Company, owned all the claims in that creek right up to Mike's claims and they also owned the claims on the other side of Mike's claims.

Before Mike owned his claim he had cut a supply of wood and stacked it on a hill (I assume on the FE company's claim.) When the dredge came through this narrow creek with a road on one side and the steep hill on the other side, the FE Company nudged the dredge into the hill because there was gold there. All Mike's logs fell down and possibly damaged his wood or got buried in his tailings. Mike figured the company owed him a settlement. The company didn't agree because Mike's logs were probably on their claim.

When the dredge was right up to Mike's claim, the big time mining company wanted to pay Mike, no doubt a pretty penny, to go through his claim. As far as I know, the dredge retired right there. I think Mike was just about as stubborn as I was.

A couple of weeks after he bought them Mike asked me if I would mind helping him check out his new claims. Of course I said yes. I was sure it would be exciting. I was a *cheechaco,* meaning I didn't have any savvy about Alaska. I was just learning.

Mike said, "Don't you have any rubber boots?"

I said, "No, what do I need them for?"

Mike said, "We'll be standing in water."

"Well, my leather boots will have to do. That's all I have."

Mike already had the boards, shovels, a pick and riffles which are small sticks about 1" square to catch the gold before it goes off the end of the box. We banked rocks and gravel to guide part of the small stream in the sluice box. We shoveled the gravel in the head of the box and let the creek stream wash the gravel and wand to the lower end of the box.

We shoveled six hours into the box and then "cleaned up." We blocked the water from going through the box, then picked out the rocks and debris and then dumped the remaining residue in a gold pan, brought it home and separated the gold from the sand.

Mike panned the gold out. He had about 4 ½ oz. of gold that he shared with me. That was worth about $95 each. Gold was worth $35 an ounce then.

I bought my dad a gold belt buckle with the raw gold I had. The buckle was covered with small nuggets. I never saw my dad wear it.

Deciding to Trap

My parents were still working on the Alaska Highway, now at Gardner Creek on the American side. They had become acquainted with a couple who were trapping in the area and wanted to sell their trapping outfit. I decided to buy it. I purchased enough food to get me started. I also bought a trail parka, warm gloves, wolf mitts, socks, and most importantly, a big pair of mooseskin moccasins. I took my Duluth backpack, rifle, and sleeping bag and headed to Fairbanks, traveling via O'Hara bus, a small bus company that serviced people wanting to go to the border. Gardner Creek was three hundred miles or so southeast of Fairbanks and about twenty miles from the Canadian border.

If I were going to number my stupid decisions in some sort of order, I would say that going trapping in September, without knowing how to go about it and without a cabin or a stick of winter wood cut, would rate as the second dumbest thing I ever did. I visited my folks for a couple of days while I tried to find a place to stay for the winter. My parents introduced me to the trappers, Tom Young and his wife, Irene. I paid them $300 for the trapping equipment. I received three hundred #1 muskrat traps, eight #44 beaver traps, four #4 Newhouse traps for wolf, some stretching boards, and a few other miscellaneous items.

It was Tom who suggested I check into an abandoned pipeline camp just a mile or so from Gardner Creek for a place to live. The camp was built after the Alaska Highway was completed, to provide headquarters for a crew laying a three-inch pipeline. All the frame buildings were pretty well stripped of windows, doors, and siding, leaving only the framework and roof intact.

There was a small Quonset hut that might be made livable. Someone had been living in it not too long before. I thought that I could fix it up. There was a partition in the middle so I'd only have to heat half of it. The two windows were in fairly good shape. I stuffed some rags in the edges.

I felt somewhat uneasy about moving into the building without permission, even though it looked like anything of value had already been carted off. The pipeline was still in operation, and there was a pumping station up the road a few miles, so I decided to go see the folks there. They gave me the name of a man in Whitehorse that I could write to. I wrote to him, explaining the situation and hoping that I'd get a positive reply. I never heard back. Really, the only thing that made the Quonset livable at all was an old barrel stove. I managed to find enough stove pipe to make it work.

Becoming a Trapper

It looked like I would be snug as a bug in a rug -- I could find some dry wood. I found a small pile of cut wood that had been cut for the camp and there were many board scraps for kindling. As I sat alone in the Quonset hut, reality started to surface, and I began to think that it was going to be a very long winter. Although my parents weren't far away, and I could visit once in awhile, I couldn't stay with them in the Alaska Road Commission camp. The weather was cooling off fast, and Alaska was getting plenty of snow.

Part of my new gear was a light trail ax and a Swede saw. Cutting wood was my main chore all winter. I wasn't bored. I was too busy looking for wood, cutting it into lengths that I could carry back on my shoulder, and then sawing it up to stove-size lengths.

One day it was snowing hard, but it hadn't gotten very cold. I decided that I'd better come up with some kind of plan and figure out where I would go trap. There were two groups of Indians living nearby, the Northway Indians to the north and the Scotty Creek Indians to the south. I didn't want to trap in their territory so I thought I would start right from my camp and go east. (Years later I understood that all of that land was theirs, but at the time it didn't look that way to me.)

I took off on my snowshoes with the light ax and started cutting a trail that I believed would be wide enough if I ever got a dog team. I planned to head for some hills that I had seen three or four miles to the east. The area between camp and the hills was mostly black spruce, a short tree that grows in dense thickets but never seems to reach great size. I worked on the trail most of the day, whacking off little trees where I had to and moving them to the side, blazing a tree on both sides within sight of each other so I could follow the trail either way.

After working on the trail all day, I came to someone's snowshoe trail. *Gosh*, I thought, *I'm really not alone out here.* Then I noticed my fresh blaze markings on the trees. I had just made a big circle. I still don't understand why life's lessons are often time consuming and agonizing, like this one was. From then on, I used my compass and picked land marks.

Crossing that dense forest in the snow was like being in a sack. The snow became heavier and more frequent, and the snowshoes became really important. The temperature steadily dropped, making every element of survival important.

My commercially made snowshoes were good, but a lot heavier than I needed. Walter Northway, the Chief of the Northway Indians, made snowshoes. I'd seen some of his work and I really wanted a pair. I ordered two pairs at $20 a pair. He finished them in a month, and they were beautiful. The bibish (moose rawhide filling) was delicately cut, and very even, making the snowshoes a work of art. The show is so dry in midwinter, it was easy on the snowshoes which I started using immediately.

I saved my commercial snowshoes for the spring when the snow would freeze a hard crust at night, then thaw during the day, a condition that is tough on webbing and frames. To improve my outfit for trapping, I bought some Canadian socks large enough to go over other socks without being tight. Conventional socks can be a size 14 but they're only longer than the size 11, not wider, and they get tighter and tighter if you add one on top the other. I had a good outfit now so I thought it was about time that I started trapping.

It was now December and the weather was getting extremely cold. The temperature dropped continually, -50 below zero, then -60, then -70. I wondered when it would stop. I didn't dare go far from my camp, but I thought it would be a good way to test my clothing to see if I could stay warm. I took hikes on the road and trails that I knew, staying out about four hours at a time. By the time that I returned, I had to do all sorts of movements to rebuild the heat in my body. I knew that I would have to wait for a break in the weather before I could head out alone on the trail.

On days that warmed up to -30 below, I ventured out farther and set a few traps. I experimented with different methods, but I had difficulty remembering where my traps were. I had to train myself to be more observant, to make a set at a place where there was a good natural landmark or a tree I could recognize. It was all part of the learning process. Until I learned that, I didn't come close to catching anything.

Bill Northway Takes Me to the Village

I was out on one of my exercise excursions when I met a fellow on the trail, about twenty miles from Northway. The old-timer introduced himself as Bill Northway, Chief Walter Northway's brother. He asked if I wanted a ride to the village, and I decided to go. He stopped at his cabin on the way, proudly showing me his steambath.

I told him that it was a lot like a Finnish sauna. It was simple, but it was beautifully made. A network of willows bent over and fastened to the structure was covered with canvas, and the ground was covered with clean wild hay. I could see that it must work very well. Finns use a stove to heat the rocks, but Bill's rocks were heated on a campfire and then carried in and laid in the center of the hay. It only took a small quantity of water to make steam, and the dome circulated the steam nicely. I made one just like it one time later and it worked very well.

Bill asked me what I wanted to do—go visiting or go to a dance. He said if he rang the school bell, all the village would come to the school for a dance.

"Let's have a dance," I said quickly. "I haven't done anything like that in a long time."

I suggested that we go up to Nellie Kelly's and get a bottle of liquor. Bill drove his team up to Nellie's and I made the purchase. After we left, I noticed that the seal on the bottle had been tampered with. It looked like coffee grounds were floating around in the bottle. Nellie must have made two bottles from one. I didn't ask Bill to go back. Nellie was a good-hearted old girl, hacking out a living the best way that she could. I worked for her cutting wood for a couple of days. I was in darn good shape but she handled the heavy green birch logs better than I could.

We got down to the school, a small log structure, just one room for classes and one room for the teacher's quarters. Bill rang the school bell. I stashed the bottle of liquor out in the snow. Soon, people started drifting in, young and old dressed in their best. Three men sported white shirts, and the ladies had pretty skirts and blouses. All wore beautifully beaded mooseskin moccasins. I adored the aroma from the smoked mooseskin. It made the occasion unique.

When there were enough people to start the dance, a hand-cranked phonograph and some well-used records provided the music. I hadn't danced what I called the <u>mukluk</u> or moccasin shuffle before, but I soon caught on. The group would glide gently with the music, slightly moving their bodies to keep time. It was nice. When the old phonograph started to slow down, the dancers slowed down. Then someone wound it up again, and everyone danced faster to keep up the pace.

Chief Northway had several daughters. The one that caught my eye was Cecilia. All the girls were pretty, but Cecilia had that something special. I tried to dance with her every chance I got. Before the night was over, the liquor had its effect, and I asked her to marry me. She politely told me she wasn't ready to get married and that she thought married life was too hard. Meanwhile, I thought about how to carry on a courtship when we lived so far apart.

After a few hours of the dance, there was a break and Chief Northway gave a speech. He made many gestures with his arms, and sometimes his feet, and by his voice I could tell he was very excited. Everyone focused on him, and I wished that I knew what he was saying. I leaned over toward Silas, who was a thirty-five year old Atahabaskan man I had become acquainted with, and whispered in his ear.

"What's he saying? Is he declaring war?"

Silas grinned and whispered back, "No! He's telling the young people to take care of themselves, and to be good and honorable, and that some of them will be the leaders someday."

After the break, I played a few tunes on my harmonica. I was pretty good at "Little Brown Jug" and "Pretty Red Wing." But after a few rounds for the dancers, I was winded. We went back to the phonograph. The music and dancing went well into the night. The school teacher, quartered in the adjoining room, got disgusted with the noise. He asked everyone to quiet down because he couldn't sleep, and he didn't have any interest in joining the dance. Everyone continued dancing. Suddenly a door slammed, and there was a big commotion on the porch. The teacher was throwing all the parkas out in the snow. Things simmered down a little then, and people started leaving one by one. As I left, I realized that Nellie Kelly did us a big favor by watering down the liquor. I didn't know where I'd stay for the night until the Sam family were kind enough to take me to their place to sleep.

That night, as the village slept, the airport hanger burned to the ground.

The next day, I walked the twenty miles back to my camp, regretting that I'd bought the liquor. I learned alcohol was bad news for the Eskimos and Indians. I never drank alcohol after 1947.

I kept experimenting at trapping, but nothing exciting was happening. The weather stayed cold, often thirty to forty-five degrees below zero, and I wondered if that had something to do with the animals not moving much. I was in a quandary, wondering if I was wasting my time, when I received a message from Silas. He wanted me to meet him on his trail, at a certain time on a certain day, and he agreed to take along his trapline.

1923 Hilda Savela and son Bruce

1927 Raynold Irvin Savela in his uncle's mailbox

1928 Bruce Savela (left) and Raynold Irvin Savela. As young men, both would serve in the Navy in WW II.

1932 Raynold Irvin Savela and his dog Nikki compete in a Half-Team Dog race.

1942 Mile Marker 1146.6 sign marks the Edith Creek area, where Ray first worked in Alaska.

1942 ff Ray Savela (left) and Bruce Savela both served in the Navy during WW II.

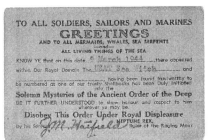

1942 Crossing the equator in WWII.

1946 Ray responded to Alaska's call and went north up the Alaska Highway. Mile Marker 0 on the Alaska Highway, Dawson City Canada.

1946 Flood in Fairbanks. John and Hilda Savela's house flooded. The Amouaks camped on the lumber pile.

1940's Amouak family pictures. Lucy; Lucy's siblings; Lucy's father
Oliver Amouak

1947 Lucy Amouak and Ray Savela on their wedding day

1940's Olga and Oliver Amouak, Lucy's parents.

1950's Lucy with Judy and Jerry, the two children in the family during the Trip Outside of '52.

1967 approx. Ray's father John, a friend, Ray's son Jerry, and Ray's mother Hilda after a moose hunt.

NORTHERN TERMINUS OF THE "ALCAN" MILITARY HIGHWAY TO ALASKA

THIS HIGHWAY WAS CONSTRUCTED DURING WORLD WAR 2 AS A MILITARY SUPPLY ROUTE TO SUPPLY INTERIOR ALASKA MILITARY INSTALLATIONS AND AIRFIELDS ENROUTE. IN MARCH OF 1942, SEVEN ARMY REGIMENTS ASSISTED BY 47 CONTRACTORS AND THE PUBLIC ROADS ADMINISTRATION BEGAN CONSTRUCTION OF THE "PIONEER ROAD" WHICH, WORKING FROM DELTA JUNCTION SOUTH AND DAWSON CREEK NORTH, WAS COMPLETED WHEN THE CREWS MET AT SOLDIER'S SUMMIT ABOVE THE SOUTHERN SHORE OF KLUANE LAKE, YUKON TERRITORY, IN NOVEMBER OF THAT YEAR.

AT THE PEAK OF CONSTRUCTION, 77 CONTRACTORS EMPLOYED OVER 15,000 MEN AND USED OVER 11,000 PIECES OF ROAD BUILDING EQUIPMENT. TOTAL CONSTRUCTION COST FOR 1422 MILES WAS $115,000,000.

1965-1968 Ray was named mayor of Delta Junction, the terminus of the Alaska Highway, Mile Marker 1422.

1972 Trip Outside. Ray and Lucy took this VW with a roof-top tent south to pick up the doctor's truck.

1972 Trip Outside. Lucy stands in the cab of the doctor's truck. The VW with the tent on top is in the bed of the truck.

1972 Ray designed the logo for Delta Junction's new fire truck obtained with coupons.

June, Jewel, John (1953-1982), Jerry, Judy (back); Lucy, granddaughter Regina, Ray

Lucy, Ray's Tundra Rose

1987 Looking for a wife, Ray spotted Pat Bergh on a bench at the
High School Reunion (far right)

Pat Bergh in Donnelly Lake.

Pat Bergh examines abandoned equipmeńt in Alaska

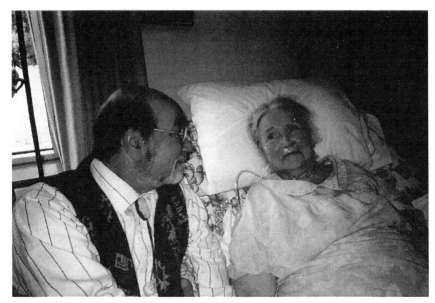

1995 Ray Savela with his mother Hilda the day before she died.

Lucy's land distribution from the state was the beautiful setting near Donnelly Lake which Ray frequently visited and where he proposed to Pat Bergh.

Pat Bergh and the golden nugget ring Ray carried for years. On the
'"witness" rock.

Oil portraits of Ray Savela and Pat Bergh, by Murray Oliphant

Ray selected his tombstone from a Minnesota quarry near scenes of his childhood and had it engraved to his specifications to be transported to Alaska. Ray's chosen epitaph: "Thank you Eskimo and Indian for sharing your land with me."

TRAPPER

1946 Trapline, Shavings, and Small Wood

It was 35 below when I walked the seven miles on the Alaska Highway to where my friend Silas and I had agreed to meet. I was just in time to see him coming up the trail with the dogs. Silas put pressure on the brake to stop the dogs and placed the anchorhook to a small tree. He greeted me, shook my hand and then introduced his trapping companion, a young fellow nineteen years old, just two years younger than myself. His name was Abraham.

I started to set my Duluth pack down when Silas said, "Let's cross road before we load your stuff. Dogs will be ahead in narrow trail."

When Silas went to the back of the sled to unhook the anchor, the dogs started barking and snarling with gusto, with one exception, Dennis, who was waggling his tail. I was sure he would be my friend. The lead dog was only half the size of the other three dogs, but he was truly a leader. The dogs were all very lean and not as strong as well-fed working dogs should be. Because these dogs had been loaned to Silas by different people, they may not have worked as a team before, but the dogs traveled well together.

Though it was 35 below, it was much warmer than it had been a couple of weeks earlier when the temperature was in the -70's. Silas had shot a moose during that cold spell, but the rifle bolt broke off in his hand when he thrust a shell into the chamber.

Silas opened the canvas cover on his toboggan so I could load my grub and gear. I was surprised the toboggan didn't have much of anything in it. His supplies were meager, just a rifle, a few traps, and a couple of other items. I didn't see any food at all. My outfit included my sleeping bag, light frying pan, tea, coffee, salt, pepper, tin plate, tin cup, skinning knife, spoon, toilet paper, etc. Ma had offered to cook a batch of beans and a pot of spaghetti and I had put the food in bowls to freeze. After it was frozen, I wrapped the two dozen meals in wax paper. I thought it would make a meal in a hurry, along with hardtack, butter, coffee, or tea. Silas secured the canvas and tucked my 300 Savage rifle on the outside so it would be handy if needed.

Running the Trapline

The accumulated snow averaged between 2 ½ and 3 feet. I didn't see a sign of the trail after we traveled beyond the trees. Silas' sled was actually a tobaggon built much like a conventional dog sled, except it had a flat bottom instead of runners. Silas said it was much better for breaking trail after a fresh snow. No one rode the sled; nevertheless it was slow going. We had to break trail all the way. Silas took the lead so he could check his traps as we traveled. I followed Silas, stepping between his snowshoe tracks with my snowshoes. Abraham followed me with the team.

Silas took side trips 10 or 15 feet off the main trail to check his traps. If he caught anything, he would take the catch out carefully so the trap didn't damage the fur. If the trap was snapped for some other reason, he would reset it. I couldn't understand how he found his traps. I didn't see anything marked and many places didn't have a tree to blaze.

I looked back periodically to see if Abraham was doing OK. Once when I looked back he was about an eighth mile behind me and he wasn't moving forward. I turned around and backtracked to see what the trouble was. Abraham was off the main trail, and one dog was caught in a trap. Abraham had tried to open the trap, but he gave up because he thought the dog might bite him.

The dog in the trap was Dennis, the one that waggled his tail at me. I talked to Dennis to sooth his nerves before I gently opened the trap. After Dennis pulled his foot out, I gently rubbed his paw and didn't feel anything broken. Dennis licked his foot and then my hand, as if to say thanks. I think by the time I got to Abraham, Dennis' foot was numb, making it easier for me to remove the trap than when Abraham had tried. We headed up the trail again with Dennis limping along. Before the day was over he had almost recovered.

Silas was kind to the dogs, perhaps more so because they were not his. He cut a few spruce boughs for each dog and placed them on the snow for their beds along the trail.

Camp One

Silas' camps were established in the fall. His 10' x 12' white canvas wall tents were already set up, including a light sheetmetal tent stove. Other things were already there: a couple of tin cans with a wire bail, light frying pan, matches, candles, etc. Silas hauled his axe and small Swede saw from camp to camp. He had prepared the sites with a few standing dead trees 4" – 5" in diameter. The bark had been stripped a couple of feet or more to kill the tree. This added to the supply of dry firewood. The camp sites were about eight or ten miles apart, depending on the supply of wood and other factors, such as daylight. During the Winter Solstice there is only about 2 ½ hours possible sunshine. There had to be time to check and reset the traps before darkness was upon us.

At our first camp, we got a nice fire going, melted snow, and then placed the frozen food in the frying pan to thaw and heat. It didn't take long before we were eating our supper. After we were through eating the beans and hardtack, Silas went outside and started digging the snow with one snowshoe. I wondered what he was up to. When the snow was cleared from his cache, he removed the moss and sticks from the hole he uncovered and pulled up a birchbark basket loaded with low bush cranberries called lingonberries that were in beautiful condition. Silas put some berries in the frying pan along with water and sugar, cooked them, and, presto, we had a delicious dessert.

In the morning we cooked oatmeal and coffee. When we were through eating the first course, I decided to cook some cranberries. Silas said no. Of course I asked him why. Silas said, "Old people say no eat cranberries in morning." He didn't know why. He was just respecting the elders' rules, or he may have wanted to conserve the berries for a later date. We prepared shavings and small wood to be ready to start a fire on our return trip. We gave the dogs a treat and headed for Camp Two.

Camp Two

We had a good meal prepared from my quick frozen beans, hardtack and coffee. The warmth from the stove was lovely and with time on our hands, this put us in a good mood for story telling. Many things puzzled me and I thought now was a good time to ask Silas about a few things.

"Silas, how do you know where the trail is since it snowed eight or ten inches since you were here three or four weeks ago?"

"First trail is froze. When off trail I feel it. Sometimes drifted, but I find it."

"How do you keep snow from freezing on your traps?" Silas showed me the paddle he had in the sled. It was something like the flat wood bread-lifter my mother used, only much smaller.

Silas said, "Be careful. Cut size snow you want, lift carefully and gently slide off over trap. It not freeze." Snow is dry in interior Alaska. That's why his system worked.

Before we left Camp Two, we checked the mouse-proof containers, including the candles and matches. There was enough shavings and small wood to start a fire on our return trip. Abraham had the dogs harnessed to the sled, so we were ready to head for Camp Three.

Camp Three

There was something special about Camp Three. It was located in higher country where there was an abundance of black spruce groves, the home of the dark martin. Before World War II, their hides would bring over a hundred dollars each. Now a good price was $40.00 across the board. Silas was better prepared in this camp because he spent more time there. He even had a huge pot like you would use for canning.

The weather was changing, getting much colder. We didn't have a thermometer, but we knew the signs. Silas decided it was too cold to run his traps the next day, so we cut more wood, taking advantage of what daylight was left. The tent started to frost inside, a sign that the temperature was dropping steadily. Our main chore now was dragging more dry wood into camp and cutting it up to fit the stove.

After three boring days, Silas decided he was going to check one trap that wasn't very far away. Abraham and I said OK, we'd take care of the camp. After Silas left, we cut a little more wood, melted more snow, and did a few other chores. Then Abraham said, "Let's take the dogs and get a load of moose meat. I know where it is. It's only about three miles from here." I agreed.

We took the axe and a burlap sack along in case we could get at the suet and that was about all. Abraham knew how to find the trail, so he had no trouble locating the moose. It was so frozen it was like a piece of iron. I was well aware that "strong" things can break when it's extremely cold. If the axe handle should break, or even the blade itself, we would be in big trouble. We managed to cut off about 200 pounds of meat. We loaded it in the sled and lashed it down.

We were ready to go up the first and steepest hill, but we barely got started when our little lead dog was having a problem. His harness collar was much too large for him and towing this heavy load made it chaff his shoulders. Luckily we had the burlap sack along. I stuffed the sack between his shoulders and the collar to fill in the void. It helped a lot. We were making such poor progress I thought the moose must have been more than three miles from camp. With the four dogs, Abraham and myself, it was a struggle to climb that first big hill. Abraham was not strong. His health was a problem -- he was infected with tuberculosis.

Even as hard as we worked we were getting colder. If we just kept moving, we'd be OK after we'd conquered the big hill. The rest of the way would be much easier. When we made our last turn within sight of our camp, we could see smoke drifting straight upward from the stove pipe. Not a breath of air changed its course until it reached about 75', then made a 90 degree bend and slowly drifted away. Abraham and I were ecstatic to see Silas was back and had a fire going.

We took care of the dogs and went inside the tent to greet Silas. We knew right away that something was amiss by Silas' expression and reaction to us. Abraham asked him if he caught a martin. Silas ignored the question.

"You no fix shavings and little wood for me to start fire. My hands almost froze. Cannot hold match. Almost didn't make fire. You boys no listen to me!" That's all Silas said. It was a lesson that I'll never forget. Abraham and I had overlooked the very basics of survival in the Arctic. We knew better than to leave without preparing fire wood. It was a mistake that could have cost Silas his life. He could have easily frozen to death before he managed to start a fire if he'd been alone.

The atmosphere was cool and quiet for about thirty minutes while Abraham and I hung our heads sulking. We both knew we made a bad mistake that could have been disasterous. Facing the facts, we all made a mistake. Silas said he was going to check one trap. He actually checked several traps, because he came back with five martin. I know he did this because it was a long trip to the village and back, and I know it was way overdue to check his traps. And he was depending on coming back to a warm camp. Abraham and I accepted it that we were most wrong.

After the silence subsided and we had plenty of time to digest what we had done, Silas asked, "You get meat. You almost freeze too?"

We both responded, "Yes! We sure did." The subject never came up again and Silas recovered his good nature.

The food I had furnished was long gone, so we started eating the moose. We'd whack off a big chunk of the frozen meat and cook it in the large pot. The meat was so tough I had a hard time eating it. Silas and Abraham didn't seem to have any trouble. They would cut off a big piece, take it in their mouths and cut the remaining meat off with their skinning knives, chew the moose meat awhile and then swallow it.

While we were out scrounging wood and dragging the moose to the tent, a couple of dogs managed to get inside and ate the butter we had cached away. I didn't blame them. The moose was shot in such cold weather that it started to freeze before the insides had a chance to cool slowly. As hungry as the dogs were, they had a hard time chewing pieces off the carcas lying outside the tent.

Getting wood kept us busy for the next few days while waiting for the temperature to change. It was cold in the tent even when the stove was snorting away full blast. We left our warm clothes on all day and slept with them on as well. When the tent was as warm as it was going to get, Silas would tell me stories.

"How do young people in the village get married, Silas?"

"If two young people want to get married, they tell the council and it will be arranged. If a girl goes to the council and tells them, 'So and So played with me,' the council gets hold of the boy and tells him that he has to marry the girl and support her and the baby. Ha! Ha! Abraham know all about that, hah! Abraham, you know!" Abraham didn't say a word.

"What if you had a man in the village that did a bad thing, what does the council do?"

"In old days council listens to both side of story. If council convinced person guilty, maybe ordered to leave village forever. If he go to other village, maybe not welcome. They think he did bad things. Be like man without country."

I slept closest to the stove, so I'd start the fire in the night. My sleeping bag wasn't doing so hot. This bag was issued to me when I worked on the Alaska Highway. The down had shifted, so there were places where the inner cloth and the outer cloth were touching. Silas and Abraham had only a couple of blankets. I didn't see how they slept at all.

After the fire was out a couple of hours, Silas would shout, "You cold, Ray?"

I'd yell back "No," although I was.

A few minutes later Silas would repeat, "You cold, Ray?"

"I'm fine, Silas."

Finally Silas shouted, "Ray, I'm freezing. Get the fire started."

Our supplies were getting low. Silas had saved all his cigarette butts and stored them in a Prince Albert can for later use, so he could roll his own with the cigarette papers he brought along. We used up the last candle, so Silas made a little lamp by twisting a piece of cloth for a wick to lay on the edge of a jar cover that held the bacon grease. It worked very well. We would add wood to the stove while Silas continued his stories.

Once as he was talking, he heard a noise outside our tent. He curved his hand around his ear to hear better and then put his finger to his lips to silence Abraham and me. Silas reached for his rifle very cautiously and carefully leaned forward to open the tent door flap about an inch. He placed his rifle barrel through the narrow opening, pulled the trigger and BANG!!! the gun went off.

Abraham and I were frozen in the positions we were sitting in, awestruck. What the heck did Silas shoot at? It was a caribou. We had to leave it outside until it was thoroughly bled, and then we pulled it in without leaving the tent. Abraham and I finally relaxed and helped Silas cut up part of the caribou.

Silas said, "Plenty meat now."

Abraham and I gathered snow in the big pot so Silas could start cooking the head. After the head boiled a couple of hours, the hair started slipping into the broth.

I asked Silas, "Why didn't we skin the head first?"

"Hair come off easy this way." Then he started fishing the hair out. When we decided the head was cooked, Silas gave me the nose. He said it was the best. I wasn't as fussy about food by this time, so I ate the nose. After gaining some experience, I would later decide that I liked the tongue and brains better.

Breaking Camp

By this time, about ten days of waiting, the weather hadn't changed one bit. Abraham started complaining, "not enough grub," although there was plenty. I thought Abraham was lonesome for his family. About two days later, Abraham decided to go home to the village. Silas didn't discourage him. He was well aware that Abraham could make that trip by himself. After all, Silas had been his tutor ever since he was a little boy, and he had taken his lessons seriously.

Silas and I stayed in camp hoping it would warm up. I still missed having something to read and a deck of cards, but on the other hand the stories I heard from Silas were worth far more than books and cards.

"How do you make sinew?" I asked Silas.

Silas took a piece of caribou muscle, backstrap, down from the peak of the tent where he had hung it to dry. He showed me how the fine strands came apart ready to sew with.

The next day Silas became fidgety, not settling down to tell stories, and it was still too cold to run traps. Nothing seemed to be going right. I wondered why Silas was acting so strangely. Then I noticed him looking in the empty Prince Albert can as if it might have seeded and grown more tobbaco. It was obvious this was his breaking point.

Silas said, "In two days we go home." We didn't wait two days. Silas decided to go home the next morning. I made shavings and small wood, put matches in the Prince Albert can, candle butts handy. Silas would not freeze his hands on a future trip. I did that chore myself to let Silas know that I learned a lesson. He didn't say anything, but he was watching me.

We had been gone twelve days. Many hours early before sunup we prepared to make our trip home. We decided not to stop at the other two camps or to build a fire to make tea. Now that we decided to leave, we were both anxious to go home. Silas had caught eight Martin, worth $40 each. We loaded about a hundred pounds of moose meat and what was left of the caribou for Silas' and Abraham's families.

The trail was good so we expected to make good time. The sky was clear. The moon shone brightly. A trillion stars twinkled upon us from the heavens. Shadows appeared from the trees and snow drifts, as if an unfamiliar sun was trying to reach us. A strange phenomenon takes place when the temperature drops to the -70s and -80s. Frost starts drifting down from the sky as if by magic to warn you "Be careful. You are in the danger zone."

We didn't need snowshoes going home. The trail was frozen as firm as a cement sidewalk. Every determined step we took and every twist of the sled strained the harnesses, adding an eerie spirit sound. It was comforting to know we had two camps on our way to stop at in case we were in trouble. Thank God we didn't need them. Silas and I dog-trotted, walked fast, and kept moving.

When we reached the Alaska Highway about midnight, Silas stopped the dogs so I could get my rifle and Duluth pack. Then we bid farewell. Silas went to his village home and I walked the last seven miles down the road to my abandoned quonset hut. The moon was bright. It was easy to see so I just kept dog-trotting home. I hoped as I walked along that I had remembered to make shavings and small wood for my fire. I was so exhausted when I got home that I crawled into my sleeping bag, clothes and all.

In the morning, I went to visit my parents and let them know that I was back. They were pleased to see me. They were worried because it was so cold, dropping down to -70 degrees below zero, just a few days after we left. The winter of 1946 when we were trapping was the coldest winter I spent in Alaska in over 50 years. We had two cold snaps that ranged in the -70's which lasted eight to ten days each time with milder weather in between. "Mild" was -20 to -40 degrees. The offical weather station at Snag Yukon Territory, Canada, was about 20 miles south of the Alaska Highway ARC at Gardner Creek Camp. It recorded -84 degrees. The high country we were in could have been a few degrees warmer.

Surviving

Surviving village life is not easy. Silas' home was very humble. His house was about 20' x 20' with a wood floor, single wood walls, and canvas nailed on the outside. His only furnishing was a wood stove. I'm sure anyone raised in the same environment would have lived very much the same way. Within a year, both Silas and Abraham died. Silas tried to flag down a bus for a ride back into the village. The driver claimed he refused to let Silas board because he was too drunk. (Silas didn't bring along alcohol on the trip I shared with him. I didn't know that he had a problem with alcohol.) Silas climbed on top of the bus, fell off, and was killed. Abraham died of TB.

Late one evening, there was a loud thump on my Quonset door. I couldn't imagine who would be stopping by at that time of night. I never had company. I opened the door, and I was about to ask the man in when he hollered, "Who the hell gave you permission to stay in this building?"

I tried to be calm and asked him to step in so I could explain things. I told him that I'd written to Mr. So-and-So asking permission, but that he'd never replied.

"That's me," he said abruptly. Then he hesitated a few seconds and recalled the letter, and apologized for not answering. I offered him a cup of coffee while we discussed the problem. Before he left, everything was smoothed out. He shook my hand and told me not to worry about staying there for the rest of the winter.

A Trapping Partner

Tom and Irene showed up for a visit. Tom had sold me his trapping equipment because he wasn't feeling well. Now he was feeling much better.

"How would you like a trapping partner?" Tom blurted out. I could hardly believe my ears.

"Boy, I really need one," I said, shoving my hand towards him. "Put 'er there!" We shook hands to seal the deal. We were partners.

Tom was an experienced trapper from Oregon, twice my age. I was sure that things would go well between us. I thought that my youth and his experience would complement each other. Tom and I didn't venture very far during the end of the extremely cold winter. But it was quite an advantage to have a pickup truck to drive ten or fifteen miles to check a trap or go to the trading post. I had caught three beaver and one fox when Tom decided to come back, and I had to do a lot of walking to check the sets. And Irene's cooking was real luxury.

Tom wanted to go toward the mountains for spring beaver trapping. We decided to do some research to see if we could find any. Tom was pretty heavy, and it wasn't possible for him to lift his legs high enough to break trail, so that part was up to me. We made a few attempts to get a decent trail established. When we finally had one, we set up a small tent across the river and stashed a small outfit there. We had packed our sleeping bags, traps, and a few other things, making a very hefty load, a couple of times. It was mid-March now, and the days were getting longer. The sun felt wonderful when it was out, reflecting off the snow and tanning our faces.

"Let's leave our sleeping bags home. Mine's too heavy and I can't stay warm in it," Tom suggested one morning. He thought he could *siwash* it (sleep by the campfire). We left that morning going towards the river. We had traveled about a half hour longer than we should have to get to our tent.

"Something is wrong," Tom said. "We should have gotten to the river by now." I agreed. Tom suggested that we walk another half hour and then see what happened. It had snowed since we made our last trip, but we both had confidence that we were on our trail. We walked the extra distance.

"Tom, see those hills and cutbank?" I asked. "That's got to be the river. We couldn't see the hills and cutbank from here unless we crossed the river."

"How can that be?" Tom asked. "We couldn't have crossed the river without knowing it."

I didn't think so either, but we both knew that something had happened, and that that was the most logical thing I could think of. I dug in my packsack, taking out a compass so I could take a bearing of the hills.

"What are we going to do now?" I asked Tom.

"Let's just keep going. We'll figure out what went wrong later," he replied.

"Okay, let's go," I answered.

We were in a big open swampy country. It was a nice area to travel in the winter, but it was impossible to travel in the summer.

"Let's head for that timber," Tom said. "It looks interesting. Can you make it?"

Alaska, No Regrets

"I'll try," I said weakly. The timber was several miles away and I was really getting tired.

We headed for the timber. Tom was right. The big swampy area we had been in was the head of the creek. By the timber, it was unusually coarse ground with deep sections that looked like the ground had sunk or like a spot where a past bog burned down to gravel. The farther we went the better it looked. Finally, we reached open water and beaver houses. We decided to just make one set at each beaver house because it looked like there would be more, and we were right. We made eight sets, all at different beaver houses. That was all the traps we had so we decided it was time to head home.

Our main objective was to find a camping spot with at least one good dry tree for night wood. We went towards the hills and cutbank, mostly because we couldn't think of anywhere else to go. We moved in that direction, crossing another open section of swamp, when Tom suddenly didn't feel good, and he wasn't sure how much farther he could travel.

"Can you hang on until we find a big tree?" I asked.

"I'll try," he replied, sounding very drawn. Luckily, we spotted a big dead spruce on the edge of the swamp, just on the fringe of a timbered area.

We had a routine. Usually, we both gathered small wood to get the cooking fire going. Then, Tom cut the big tree down and sawed it into five foot lengths. We got the little fire going this time, and then Tom got started on the big tree, working only a short while before he had to quit. His belly ached, and he felt nauseated.

"Sit down on a log," I cautioned him. I promised that I'd take care of the night wood. As tired as we were, Tom couldn't eat a bite. Maybe it was the snow water. We had roasted a little beaver on the campfire, and I gave Tom the liver, forgetting about the gall. Maybe it was the liver gall.

After supper, we put a five foot log on each side of the fire and a third at a slight angle so that it didn't cut the draft off. Making a bed of spruce limbs about three feet from the fire, we put all our extra gear on top of that. I laid on top of my trail parka, wearing a wool sweater and my best socks.

Once the fire took hold and had any hot coals, it put out a lot of heat. The biggest problem was cooking your body on one side, and freezing it on the other side. It's dangerous burning up your only clothes with twenty miles to travel. That night, I burnt the back of my wool jacket. I was lucky that it was the only thing that I burnt. It seemed like we dozed off for about thirty minutes at a time before our backs were chilled. It had already started snowing before we were settled for the night. It was quite miserable. By morning, there was about four inches of fresh snow, and it was still snowing hard. Tom didn't feel very good. He couldn't eat any breakfast or drink coffee, but he did think that he could travel.

We briefly talked about which direction to go. Because of the dense forest and snow, we couldn't see any landmarks. We each thought we should go in a different direction. Luckily, I had taken bearing of the hills the day before. I scrambled to get out my compass and went by that bearing. I picked a tree as far as I could see, and after we reached it, I picked out another one.

As it turned out, it took us right to the river, and the cutbank that we had seen. Now, all we had to do was head upstream on the river until we found our trail. Tom was finally doing fine, and we became confident that we were going to make it. Along the way, we discovered what we had done wrong. The creek got wider where it entered the river, and the river had an island that divided the river and a slough.

We had crossed the river, thinking that we had zigzagged across the creek.

Tom perked up after we reached our home camp, and after he had a couple meals of his wife's good cooking. Four days later, after a good rest and cutting enough wood for Tom's wife, we headed off.

Our trail was getting better every time that we used it. And we were becoming better acquainted with the country. Our first set paid off with a big beaver.

I whooped for joy, and Tom said he hadn't seen such a big smile on my face for a long time. We decided to check all the traps, and then make camp to skin them. I told Tom I'd carry the first beaver. At the second set, we had another beaver, and the same at the third set. We had to make camp right then for that night, and we skinned the beaver by the campfire.

The next day was a repeat performance of the first. Three more beavers. Again we made camp and skinned them. The next day we only had two traps left to check, and they each had a beaver. Every trap we had set had had a beaver. We set all the traps again, one at each house, knowing that we didn't want to take more than two from a house. We did get our limit.

Tom and I had planned to trap muskrats that spring too, but for some reason, Tom and Irene decided not to stay. And I wasn't going to do it alone. Tom and I made some muskrat sets on our way to the beaver houses, and we caught forty or fifty muskrats.

In a way, I was glad that Tom decided not to continue trapping. The nature of the business was weighing on my soul, and I made a conscious decision not to trap the following winter. I knew I could trap. It would have been hard work, but much easier than the winter that I'd just endured. I'd have put up line cabins, cut my wood at each site, and stashed food and supplies. I'd learned a lot. Enough,that I knew that if I wanted to I could survive the next winter in relative comfort. Even if the weather was bad, I knew how to keep my clothing dry.

It was sad to leave. We'd worked so hard on those trails, and I knew that slowly they would fade into the landscape. But there was no way to avoid cruelty to animals in the trapping business, and that I couldn't live with. I left most of the traps out in the wilderness, all gathered together, hung in the trees. I imagined someone would find and use them someday, but I didn't care. I departed happy, knowing that the animals would be free for another year--and forever from me.

SETTLING DOWN

Harry Buhro

I said goodbye to my folks and boarded the O'Hara bus, with my Duluth pack, my Trapper Nelson Packboard, my sleeping bag, and my rifle. Only a few passengers rode the bus.

"Do you mind if I sit next to you?" a small old man asked. "I'm so happy to be back in Alaska, I just wanted someone to talk to." I was happy to have someone to talk to on the long 320 miles to Fairbanks. Harry Buhro, my new traveling companion, had been Outside (in the United States) for a long time trying to get a book published, but now he wanted to gain passage back to Russia.

"I tried to buy passage on a Swedish ship," Harry said, "and they turned me down. Can you believe that?" He considered stowing away, but quickly discarded the idea. Harry had deserted the Russian Navy in China over fifty years earlier. Now he had a strong desire to find any remnants of his family before he died. We talked about the things that I had done, but mostly we talked about Harry because I found his story so intriguing. The time flew, and I was almost sorry it didn't take longer to get to Fairbanks. I wanted to hear more about Harry.

"Where are you going to stay?" Harry asked as we got off the bus. I didn't know. Harry and I decided to go to the Fearless Bakery. We checked in for $1.50 each and went upstairs to find our room. There were two single beds, a couple of chairs and a small stand. Harry continued to talk, and I continued to ask questions.

"Your book, what is the name of it?" I asked.

"Rough Stuff and Moonlight," Harry said, his eyes twinkling. "I wrote it like a novel, but it's really about my life." He showed me a picture of himself in the Russian Navy, standing by a member of a rowing crew for the ship's captain. The different ship crews competed in rowing when they were anchored in port. Harry was wearing a rower's belt in the picture, and he looked like Charles Atlas, the bodybuilder. Even now in his mid-seventies, shrunken in stature, he still had a very thick chest.

"What are you going to do tomorrow?" Harry asked. I didn't have any plans. "Do you want to go to the University with me and look at some maps?"

"Sure," I replied, I didn't see any rush. I had plenty of time to figure out what to do next.

I checked in at the desk and asked to stay another night. "That'll be fifty cents," the lady said. "If you'd like to stay a week, it'll be $2.50 more. We charge $4.00 a week." I decided to stay a week, and so did Harry.

We went to the University of Alaska and looked at map after map. Harry ran his finger along a river and said, "I spent the winter up here in 1932." Another river was the summer of 1929, and so it went. We had a wonderful week together. This old-timer was a real gem.

"I'm going to pole my boat up and down the Chena," Harry said energetically. "I have to get in shape for my next trip." I decided it was time for me to scout around and see if I could get a job. Harry and I shook hands and promised that we would try to get in touch with each other again.

Alaska, No Regrets

Some time later, I watched an old-timer poling his long boat upstream on the Chena River, remembering that Harry had told me that he could hardly wait to get his old poling boat on the river. I was glad that Harry possessed the extraordinary spirit to carry on. But I was saddened because his time was running out. As I watched the man pole his boat, I could see the ruggedness of the old sourdough, stroke after steady stroke, fading into the distance. (I never did see Harry again, but I have his book. Occasionally, I pick it up and say, "Hi, Harry. How's prospecting?")

Artic Contractors on the North Slope

"Do you know anything about seismograph work?" the interviewer asked.

"I'm sorry, but I've never even heard that word," I replied.

"You can go to work as a bullcook," he said.

"I'd rather do anything than be a bullcook," I said honestly, hoping that I wasn't blowing my chances for a job. "Do you have any other job I could do?"

The interviewer tried to convince me that if I went as a bullcook, they would send someone to take my place after a short while, and then I could move to a different job. I held my ground because I knew I wouldn't be happy as a bullcook. He decided to send me up as a jug hustler.

The next day I flew to Borrow. I wasn't there long enough to even visit the village. Immediately, I was escorted to a small bush plane to be flown to work, about sixty miles away. I stood around, watching the plane being loaded. They kept stuffing things in, until one of the cargo handlers said, "Hey, you've got your weight limit."

"Oh hell, throw it all in," the pilot replied casually.

There were two seats on the plane: one for the pilot, and another one for the passenger. I wasn't worried about my seat until another man showed up. Word had it that he was a Navy commander, and a very important person. My nervous stomach told me that I wasn't going to get a seat.

"See if you can bend over enough to sit on the freight," the pilot told me. I got in, just behind the passenger seat, bending down as far as I could. My head almost touched my knees. "That's great," the pilot said enthusiastically. "You won't have to be there long."

The plane left the ground, went up a few hundred feet, and was off. Twenty minutes later, we landed, and the commander got off. I then rode in the seat to my final destination. The pilot landed again at a deserted looking place where two men had been dropped by mistake. The pilot didn't have room for them so I figured that he planned to pick them up after he unloaded the cargo and me.

Flying over the Arctic was incredible. Its haunting beauty gave the impression that nobody lived there or that there was anything to live on. But people did survive there. A solitary sod igloo poked out of the ground, half below and half above. The wind had blown the seal or walrus guy skylight clear. Snow drifted around the structure, and we could have passed by without even noticing it.

Soon, we landed at the camp that I was to work at, one of seven used for exploring oil that summer. The party chief waited for the plane and greeted us when we landed. I wasn't sure how far from the coast we were, but I judged about 100 miles. Our party was working in the area of the Ikpikpuk River, later moving into the Oumalik River. The country reminded me of prairie country in the winter. There weren't any trees, except for a few stunted trees along the streams.

Everything in the camp was mounted on skids, runners or tracks. The rotary drill rig was on a sled made of three-inch pipe, about twelve feet wide and thirty feet long, all closed in including the mast. There were four army surplus weasels, small track vehicles that travel well over tundra and in water. There were four D-8 Caterpillar tractors, and four 9x18 foot moveable dwellings called wanigans.

The party chief told me what wanigan I was to go to. The wanigan was 10'x20'. It was very crowded for eight men, their gear, and a stove. There wasn't any room for a table or chairs. The men either sat on a lower bunk or laid down. Sometimes, they used a cardboard box to play cards on.

Dark and dreary with the two windows covered, the air was stale. Several pair of dirty, wet socks dried on a rack above the stove. I selected an upper bunk, the only empty one. There was a little door up there, about 4" x 6", that let some fresh air in. It was so dark in the wanigan because one of the guys couldn't sleep in the light. It was already early May, and that far north it never got dark. One of the workers covered all the windows. The rest of the guys called him the mole.

The wanigan got very messy. There wasn't any organization, and nobody was in charge of housekeeping. Some of the guys threw magazines and papers on the floor when they were finished with them, along with orange peels and anything else they didn't want. I couldn't stand the filth, but I hated being the cleanup boy. I'd wait it out until someone else couldn't stand it, and then they'd clean it up. That's just the way it was.

I was assigned to help the survey crew. The job required a lot of walking, but I was still in good shape from trapping. There was still a lot of snow, and the weather was cold so I decided to put my warm underwear back on. The survey crew found places where the seismograph crew should take readings. They also plotted locations and marked good spots to cross the streams for the drill rig.

The seismograph crew consisted of a powderman, a seismograph technician, and two jug hustlers. The jugs were shaped like cereal bowls, but completely enclosed. There were about 20 jugs, and each one had a wire attached to it. The wires were laid out, 20' apart, sometimes ten each way from the shot hole and at other times all on one side.

The powderman had a little wanigan that he dragged around, and the seismograph machine, mounted in a weasel especially enclosed for that purpose. When everything was laid out correctly, the powderman had five-pound sticks of powder ready.

"1-2-3 FIRE!" he'd shout over the phone to the seismograph operator, and then he'd set off the charge. At that moment, the seismograph operator would turn on his battery-operated machine to pick up the vibrations via the jugs that recorded wavy lines on film paper about 1' wide and 3' long. From these recordings, a profile of the ground structure could be read, and it indicated if this was a promising oil structure. The drill rig drilled holes ahead of the seismograph crew, no more than one day in advance or the holes would freeze. Most of the ground had permafrost.

I liked the work. It was interesting, and I was learning every day. There were two shifts, a small one at night by the clock, though still in the sun, and the day crew. The day crew worked twelve hour days, seven days a week, except for when we moved camp, and then it was sixteen hour days. We stayed in each area for a week to ten days, sometimes longer, always looking for a camping spot that would be a good place for the supply plane to land.

With the snow gone, the exposed tundra was far too rough and wet for wheels, and too dangerous for skis. The pilots were good. As long as there was a little ice on the lake, they would skim the water with their skis until it reached an ice cake close to the beach. When they took off, they usually only had a short piece of ice 20' – 40' long. They took off full-throttle, and skimmed off the water and wet grass, never having an accident in our camp. If all the ice was gone, they depended on float planes for freight, mail and personnel, because wheel planes weren't practical for summer landing on the soggy tundra. In the summer, there were lakes, ponds, potholes, and swamps everywhere. The party chief searched for the largest lake to camp by still within reasonable distance to our work area.

One time, a Wein's Seabee landed on our closest lake. After he was already down, the pilot suspected that the lake was too small to take off from. The pilot was still willing to try if the plane was as light as possible. He wouldn't even take on a drill bit. The pilot circled the lake, making waves to brake the suction, and then gave full throttle to take off. When he saw that he was not going to make it, he cut the throttle, but it was too late. He slid 20' up on the tundra. Undaunted by the experience, he had the party chief pull the plane back in the lake with a weasel.

"Let's try it again," he said confidently. He circled, started full-throttle on the far beach. About half-way across, he tried lifting off again. This time the plane popped out of the lake like an Arctic hare.

There wasn't a concern about ecology then. Ten days or two weeks after staying in one spot as the weather was warming, our campsite became a quagmire. The moss held the water for a long time. A tractor that was stuck in August ripped up the moss, and the ground was only thawed about a foot. The track vehicles didn't tear up the moss very much, but if the moss was thawed, the go-devils, a stout sled with low timber runners, did. Whenever we moved camp, all the empty fuel barrels were left helter-skelter, as well as other garbage. Now there are strict regulation, and the oil companies have been cleaning up the mess that was left over forty years ago.

As summer neared, more signs of life became evident. I saw wolves, arctic fox, and a large covey of ptarmigan, a variety of grouse that are year-round residents in the north region. The ptarmigans become pure white in the winter. As the snow and ice disappeared, migratory birds also appeared, including snow geese and loons. The caribou migrated through the area where we were working. As far as one could see, caribou moved in every direction, scattered about in small and large groups. About 250,000 caribou migrated in the group. It was a rare and exciting sight.

Finally, I secured the job I wanted as a helper on the drill rig. The job allowed me to drive a big tractor, and part of my job was to haul water from the lakes, using a tank mounted on a go-devil. When we weren't working, we fished or explored. It seems whenever I went fishing, I'd soon become more interested in something else. One day, I found two big bones, and our party chief found a small ivory tusk about 3' long. I gave my bones to a university student who was working with us. I later found out that one bone was from a horse, and the other from an ox.

One day, I received a check and a letter from Dwain, my old mining partner. It was my share from the mine. Dwain gutted the vein and took out $13,000. His brother came up to help him. (Later Dwain's brother shot and killed him in a dispute. Maybe it wasn't so dumb that I got out.)

I was working close to 500 air miles from Fairbanks. I didn't think there would be any mosquitoes, but I was mistaken. I didn't know if they were thick at Barrow, but where we were, they were ferocious. I'd seen mosquitoes in Minnesota and Fairbanks, but they never were so thick and hung around for so long. For seven weeks, they were unbearable. Working with a net was disgusting, but when I took it off, I was convinced that I was lucky to have one.

There were so many mosquitoes, they blocked the air cleaner in one of the tractors so it wouldn't run. Blue smoke came out of the exhaust and the first gear was the only way we could move at all. The mechanic cleaned the air cleaner, checked the fuel and filters, and the tractor still wouldn't run properly. The mechanic called the head mechanic in Barrow, and together they decided that the sections that couldn't be removed were plugged, and that's why the tractor wouldn't run.

A Finn Girl

My job, like many, was located far away from any city, and in that regard, I could hardly wait for the job to end. Before I got the job with the Arctic contractors, I had met a young Finn girl named Eili, the niece of one of the men that I worked with. She was from Finland, and I tried hard to communicate with her, although she didn't speak English. Romancing in Alaska was difficult. The job was almost completed, and Artic Contractors would be letting a couple of guys go, so I volunteered. I was anxious to get back in touch with the little Finn girl.

While I was on that job, my pay was deposited in a bank in Fairbanks. I had acquired a small nest egg from a few month's work. Some of the guys that infrequently went to Fairbanks went off the deep end when they finally did get to the city, spending as much as $10,000 in a month and nearly killing themselves in the process. They didn't want the trip to be such a rarity that it became a disaster for the employee, so the contractor had enforced a new rule that said employees must go to town at least once every six months. When I got to Fairbanks, I bought some new clothes and made a down payment on a small house. I found out that the little Finn girl was staying with her uncle, about 20 miles from Fairbanks. I needed transportation quickly in a bad way.

New cars weren't available, so I shopped around. Pa offered to help me look. I shrugged off his assistance, sure that I could find a good one on my own. The first car I looked at was a 1939 Buick, a beautiful blue color. I handed over $900 cash and took the car. When I drove to the gas station to fuel up, I noticed two tires were so worn that I wasn't sure the car would make it home. I bought two new tires. When I was driving home, I saw Ma walking along the road. I proudly stopped to pick her up. Ma hopped in. When I let the clutch out, we both got a big jerk. The rough gravel streets in Fairbanks made the car sway and bounce.

"What's the matter with your car?" Ma asked.

"The shocks must be shot," I muttered. "We're bouncing on the coil springs." Still, it was a beauty.

I made one trip to see Eili. I wanted to take her to town. Her uncle insisted on coming along. The next time I went up to see her, the transmission went out. But seeing Eili wasn't important anymore. I discovered that a marriage had been prearranged for her so that she could stay in America.

The longer I stayed away from Fairbanks, the more I missed the trees, and the possibility of female companionship. I had wandered around long enough, doing things that would have been difficult if I'd been married. Some of the old-timers got along well leading a solitary life, but it's a choice everyone must make, and I knew I needed a wife and a family in my future.

Fairbanks

After coming home to Fairbanks from Barrow, I didn't need a job right away, but I was thinking about a house of my own. Bruce and

I were living in my parents' garage loft till we came up with a plan. My folks decided to sell their little house to me. It was only about 20 square feet, but at least it was a start. I put up enough money to please my folks and $150 monthly payments.

There were many original old buildings still scattered throughout the city. One of my favorites was a little coffee shop on First Ave. You could enter on First Ave and also go through a narrow hallway from Second Ave. What first attracted my attention when entering this quaint little shop was its foundation that had settled for years, causing the floor to swell up and down like a sea wave all the way to the serving counter and beyond. Another attraction was a large copper kettle that was used for heating water. It must have held at least four or five gallons.

There were many more interesting business places, and I wrote a poem about one of them, called "The Line."

About two blocks west of my special coffee shop and rooms to rent was a trading post and a small log hotel. Charlie Maine owned both. Charlie's store was one of a kind. No doubt it was born when Fairbanks became incorporated. His store was cluttered with everything, including beautiful Eskimo ivory and baleen items, and useful utensils like a chamber pot for night use.

The Line

A row of little cabins
so innocent and quaint
With tin roofs and weathered logs
and sills in need of paint.

I would see men disappear from view.
Some dressed in rugged attire.

Others were dressed in their finest Sunday dower
I wondered, what was so interesting that keeps almost an hour?

One day I got up the courage to take a little peek through a knot-hole in
the fence.
Wow! I saw ladies sitting in the window,
 displaying the almost-naked bodies,
 beckoning men with teasing little naughties.

Now I'm just a little kid.
Selling the <u>Daily News Miner</u>.
If my Ma knew I was peeking there,
she would paddle my behinder.

One day I got a bright idea,
to walk in there strong and bold.
And see if they would buy a paper.
Gosh! They were nice,
they beckoned me from the cold.

They were kind to me,
all these nice ladies wanted to buy my paper.
They said when times were better they would pay,
"For now all we can do is barter."

I went home that night
and told my Ma the great news.
Of all the papers I had sold,
 and how the nice ladies warmed me from the cold.

My Ma asked me "Where Have You Been?"
I told her of all my new customers at the row of little cabins.
They were all so poor, they couldn't afford that I get paid.
If I waited till the end of the month, they would take it out in trade.

Now for some reason my Ma got so gosh almighty mad.
I didn't see anything so bad.
It all started with a little peek.
And besides, I saw Pa go there almost every other week.
(--Author's note: This poem is not about my family. Honest.)

Flood in Fairbanks

I got a job for the winter at the Alaska Road Commission. My folks bought a sauna business on Wendel Avenue. An Eskimo family from an Indian village named Tanana moved to Fairbanks and settled right next door to my folks. My folks were only in their new place for seven weeks when the streets close to the river flooded. To help, I dug up my folks' yard all the way down to the frost attempting to build a dike, hoping that the water would crest below the dike.

As I worked at my parent's house, I saw the old Eskimo couple digging thawed dirt out of their cellar. They looked like they could use some help, so I went over and offered some assistance. Our efforts were futile. The river kept going up, and the small humble dikes broke. Ma and Pa got three foot of water in their place. The Eskimo family's small cabin was sitting on a lower lot than the surrounding property. They got water clear up to their ceiling.

My parents had a few cords of 16' wood for firing the sauna, which was tied down so it wouldn't float away. Pa told the Eskimo family that they could build a shack on the wood and stay there until the water went down and they had the cabin fixed.

An Eskimo Girl

Every day I came from my place, 4 miles out of Fairbanks, to see my folks and visit the Eskimo couple, Oliver and Olga Amouak. The Amouaks were originally from Stebbina and Unalakleet and had six surviving children out of fourteen. Frankie, Bernice, Agnes, and Ralph were still at home. The oldest, Pauline, was married and still lived in Tanana. Their daughter Lucy was in school at Mount Edgecomb. Olga told me that Lucy would be home soon.

One evening, I made my usual visit and heard that Lucy had arrived. Oliver had put up a cozy tent for her. I was dying to see what she looked like. I hung around, hoping to get a glimpse. Lucy came out of the tent, but she acted like she didn't even notice me. She looked straight ahead into the distance, and she was the cutest thing I'd ever seen.

I was trying to work on my chimney and sewer system at my small house after work on my new job at the Alaska Road Commission, but I couldn't keep my mind on the work. I'd drop my tools and head for Fairbanks. I planned to ask Lucy's Pa if I could take Lucy to a movie, but I'd get cold feet and go back home instead. One night, I decided to do it, even if it killed me. I went to Oliver and Olga's, finally blurting out, "Can I take your daughter to the movies?"

Oliver looked straight at me, thought for a few seconds, and slowly said, "I guess it'd be all right."

I waited outside while Oliver asked Lucy if she wanted to go. I paced. Maybe she had refused. "With that old man?" the high-pitched voice echoed. Lucy didn't want to go. After all, I was 23 and she was only 19.

Finally, her pa said impatiently, "Hurry up, Lucy. That neighbor boy is waiting for you." When Lucy finally appeared, we said hello to each other, and that was all. When we reached the street, I looked behind us. All Lucy's brothers and sisters were following.

"Mom wants them to go too. They got their own money," Lucy said matter-of-factly. Lucy and I didn't speak ten words to each other during the entire movie, and I don't recall what those words were. But I liked what I saw, and I hoped that she might have some feelings for me too. Lucy was working as a chamber maid upstairs of a clothing and fabric store. I didn't know a young Indian man from Tanana was courting her at the store.

I came into town every night after work, and Lucy and I went for a walk, mostly to the city dump to look at my "new" 1929 Model A Ford pickup. The Alaska Road Commission (ARC) had hauled several trucks to the dump. I asked Hank, the dumpmaster, about the trucks, and he said he'd sell me one if I let him fix it up. I bought wheels, tires, a battery, belts and anything else that was missing. The ARC knocked a hole in every engine block before they dumped the trucks. Hank repaired the hole. The pickup needed a battery, a fan belt, tires, and wheels. The hole that was knocked into the lower side of the block, Hank repaired beautifully.

That's where Lucy and I went every evening if it wasn't raining. Lucy's mom Olga always asked her how her shoes get so dusty.

"Mom, it's always dusty all the way to the dump," Lucy would say.

"Is that where Ray takes you for a walk?"

"Mom! We go there almost every evening to look at Ray's new pickup."

After I got the pickup running, Lucy and I got around a lot better.

When the pickups repairs were all completed I took Lucy for a ride with her brother and sisters. Lucy said she wanted to try to drive the truck. Her brothers and sisters were riding in the back, but I decided I'd better let her try. I didn't want her to get mad at me. This girl was really cute. I showed Lucy what she should do, and she got behind the wheel. Lucy knew how to drive dogs, but this was something entirely different. I didn't realize that she had no idea which way the pickup would go when she turned the wheel. I was a little uncomfortable when we started moving because I was certain that she was going to zigzag fast down the narrow road. I tried to keep my cool, and I didn't want to excite her by grabbing the wheel. She finally made a sharp turn to the right to correct a swerve, and we went in the ditch. I was afraid we were going to have brothers and sisters scattered everywhere, so I grabbed the wheel to get us back on the road.

Lucy and I dated about six weeks, and then I asked her to marry me. She kept me on pins and needles for a few days before finally saying "Yes." I asked Oliver for Lucy's hand, and he took his good old time about it too. Finally, he offered the perfunctory, "I guess it'd be all right."

Settling Down with Lucy

Lucy wanted to be married in a Catholic church. She was the only Catholic in her family. I would have feared a large wedding, but we didn't have the money for it anyway. Lucy said I'd have to get instructions from the priest before we could get married.

"Okay," I said reluctantly. "You know I'd do anything to marry you." But, when the time came to see Father Mac, I was scared. Fortunately, my fears were unfounded. Father Mac had baptized Lucy, and his friendly manner put me at ease. I only saw him twice before we set a date for the wedding.

The big day finally arrived, and Lucy and I were getting married at 2 p.m. I was helping Pa mix cement that day. I looked at my watch about a quarter to one.

"Pa, I'm going to have to knock off pretty soon," I said impatiently. "I'm supposed to get married at two o'clock."

"You'd better find someone to take your place at the mixer," Pa replied. There was a young man standing in the doorway watching us work.

"Can you take my place at this mixer while I get married?" I asked him. Fortunately, he agreed.

When I arrived at the house, Lucy was already dressed in a soft blue suit. I quickly put on my new suit, and we dashed over to the little white church, two-and-a-half blocks away and across the river.

"My, you kids look nice," Father Mac said. "Lets go in the church and get things ready." We hadn't invited anyone, and we didn't even have a witness.

"Are you sure that you want to get married?" Father Mac asked. "It's not too late to back out."

"I want to get married," I said emphatically. Father put on his vestments while he continued to chat.

"Do you have the rings?" he asked. We passed on that point.

"And I suppose you have a license?"

"A LICENSE! Do we need a license?" I hollered, quickly frazzled.

"Of course you do," Father Mac replied. I thought getting married in a church overcame such obstacles.

"It'll take three days," Father said. "Go to the courthouse now and apply. I'll go with you." The three of us headed for the courthouse and applied for the license.

The commissioner, Mr. Smith, said, "I'll see you day after tomorrow. We'll call today your first day."

Father went back to the church. Both very disappointed, Lucy and I went back to our folks' houses. I changed clothes and went back to work on the mixer. There wasn't anything else we could do.

On the third day, we went to pick up the marriage license. To our surprise, the commissioner wasn't there. The clerk informed us that he had driven to Circle Hot Springs and was snowed in. It was late August, and this certainly wasn't normal weather. We'd have to wait longer.

Two days later, we were passing across the bridge, Father Mac stood on the other side, waving his arms and shouting. When we got closer, we could hear what he was saying.

"I've got it! I've got it!" He had our license. "Dash home, change your clothes, and meet me back at the church," he said quickly.

"Why are you putting on your nice clothes in the middle of the day?" Ma asked suspiciously.

"Lucy and I are getting married," I said, smiling slyly. "They flew the commissioner in from Circle Hot Springs, and we have our license."

Lucy's mother had the same questions as my mother, and Lucy's mother and all the brothers and sisters, followed us to the church. Father Mac had started to get ready in the church, and then he decided that it would be a better idea if we went to the little chapel in the hospital. On the way over, he asked two people to be our witnesses. Later, I was telling some friends that Father Mac picked up a nurse and a janitor to be our witnesses. Lucy corrected me, "That lady was a nurse alright, but that man was the head pastor of the church!"

We used the last few dollars I had for a honeymoon, taking a train to Mt. McKinley for three days. It was a glorious time, especially with no brothers and sisters trailing behind us. I made many mistakes in my life, but marrying Lucy, my Tundra Rose, wasn't one of them. We raised five beautiful children together: Jerry, Judy, Jewel, John and June. The fact that we managed to keep our heads above water and raise a beautiful family is worth more than all the gold in Alaska.

Married Life

The ARC paid the lowest wages around, but it was steady work. I soon discovered that married life wasn't as easy as I thought it would be. It was nip and tuck to meet our bills every month. The Northern Commercial Company owned us for quite a while.

The first October after we were married, we heard that the dog salmon were coming up the river to Delta. I bought a thirty-foot gill net. Lucy's folks and Lucy and I headed for Delta. We got a pickup load of fish. I don't know if it was legal to catch them or not, and I didn't bother to ask anybody. We didn't realize that we were close to where they spawn, and some had already spawned and others were just waiting around to spawn. The salmon were not the best eating, but they didn't taste bad if you used plenty of catsup. The fish lacked flavor, but besides bread, tea, and coffee, they were the mainstay food for us and Lucy's folks that winter.

Times were hard. Once someone gave us some strong caribou that had been shot during the rut. The meat was too strong for them or their dogs, but Lucy fixed it. "Don't tell the kids," Lucy told me firmly, "but I found worms in the meat. I think I got them all out."

Car in Winter

I learned how to keep a vehicle running. At night, I'd take the battery in the house and drain the water from the radiator. Then I'd go outside and jack up the rear wheel. In the morning, I'd try to get it started plenty early, in case it wouldn't start. I allowed enough time to walk four miles to work if I had to. Taking a shovel of hot ashes from the barrel stove, I'd slide it under the engine. While that was heating, I'd put the battery in, and when I was finally ready to try to start the car, I'd put hot water in the radiator. If it started, I'd put it in low gear to loosen the transmission and rear end, and then I was ready to go. When we ran out of gas money, I walked to work.

As time went on, I learned many ways to winterize my car and get it started, even at seventy degrees below zero. If it was really cold, I'd have to drive slowly and give the tires a chance to warm up and get round. Sometimes, if I was running late for work and drove too fast, I'd find pieces of rubber flying off the tires. Rubber shatters at sixty-three degrees below zero if abused.

Living with the Amouaks

Lucy and I had other troubles. The pot-burner oil stove sooted and carboned up, and suddenly quit burning at -40 degrees below. I had to take the stove apart to clean it, a nasty job. My father-in-law offered to let us stay at his place until there was a break in the weather until we could fix the stove.

We moved in with the six of them, squeezed into a little one room cabin, about 14' x 20'. It was very crowded. They didn't have any room for storage, or any closets, so extra clothing was hung wherever there was room. But it was typical for an Eskimo family to offer help, even when they were struggling themselves.

Lucy's folks were having to learn a new lifestyle in Fairbanks. Oliver didn't know about unions yet, and nobody knew that he was a capable carpenter. Olga was a master skin sewer. She couldn't read or write, but she knew how to measure the old-fashioned way, with her hands and arms. A little money came in from her sewing. The oldest boy sold the Fairbanks Daily News Miner.

Lucy's parents found out that they had to pay for many things in Fairbanks that they got in Tanana for merely the energy and the skill. They now had to buy fuel (coal or wood), buy water, and pay to dispose of sewage. The honey-wagon came around once a week, and it cost $1.00 a bucket to get rid of toilet waste. Water was sold by the bucket, and it was cheaper by the barrel.

At Tanana, Lucy's parents used creek water. In the winter, they cut ice in the Yukon River and used the dogs to haul the ice to their ice house for cooling summer water. They hauled all their fire wood with the dogs, and they put up ten tons of fish for themselves and their twenty dogs. They were able to hunt for moose and caribou that could be hauled home by boat or with the dogs.

And at Tanana, they had room for a big garden. Oliver earned some cash cutting wood for the sternwheelers and hauling mail from the airstrip to the post office. If a sternwheeler was left at Tanana for the winter, Oliver was paid to be the caretaker of the vessel. In time life became easier for Lucy's folks in Fairbanks as they became acquainted and people realized their skill.

That winter had its unexpected rewards. Lucy's folks won the Eskimo Dance Contest and received a free trip to Seattle, all expenses paid. After that trip, and the publicity, Alaska Air Lines flew Oliver and Olga all over the United States, Europe, and Japan to promote Alaska.

The Dancer Dale Hall

A young lady named Dale Hall heard about Lucy's parents' dancing and got in touch with them while Lucy and I were still staying there. Dale was a dancer at one of the local nightclubs, the Rendezvous. She asked Oliver and Olga to teach her a few Eskimo dances, and she said that she would pay them. It was a great opportunity for Lucy's parents to earn some extra money. They set up a schedule to teach Dale the dances. Dale came over three or four times a week to practice. Olga showed her the motions, and Oliver sang and beat out the rhythm on his drum. It was tight quarters in the cabin, barely enough room for the three of them to perform. Lucy and I, and the four kids sat and watched. Dale didn't seem to be bothered by our presence. She was very determined to learn the dances.

The dance lessons went on for several weeks, well after Lucy and I got the stove fixed and returned home. Finally the day came when Dale would perform the authentic Eskimo dances that she'd recently learned. Lucy's mother made her a cloth dancing parky to match her own, and Lucy's father sold her a set of seven dancing masks that he had carved from driftwood. The masks were beautifully made. The fox mask had a mouth that opened and shut when it was manipulated by the wearer's mouth. There was a special mask for the crazy boy dance, the seal hunt dance, and others.

The "big" night arrived, and Dale invited Lucy and me to be there to watch her and Lucy's folks perform. I was leery about going. I knew a place like that would require money. Lucy had never been to a nightclub. She was certain that we wouldn't have to spend any money. I did want to see the dance, and I decided to go to please everyone. I calculated how far my dollar bill would go, knowing that it wouldn't go very far.

The show didn't begin until 9 p.m. I stalled Lucy as long as I could. We arrived about 8 p.m. and picked out a table with a good view of the stage. Lucy's folk's were already there with Dale. As soon as we were seated, my worst fear was confirmed. A cute little waitress shuffled over with a tray. "What do you want to drink?" she asked.

"We're okay for now," I blurted. Every ten or fifteen minutes she shuffled back to check again. Finally, I decided I'd waited long enough. The next time the waitress appeared, I ordered two colas, straight. When she returned with a thimble full of cola, and the rest ice, I handed her my dollar bill, hoping that it would be enough. Thankfully, she didn't ask for any more.

"Isn't that lady ever going to bring us some change?" Lucy asked thirty minutes later.

"Honey, we're darn lucky it didn't cost any more," I said. We sipped on the glass of ice for a long time. The waitress came over with a tray of food. Lucy and I were certain she'd made a mistake.

"Compliments of Dale," the waitress said. Now, I started to relax and enjoy myself. The waitress didn't bother us anymore. She now knew that we were there to see the dancers.

"Good evening, ladies and gentlemen. We have a nice show for you tonight. Our regular band will be playing your favorite tunes. And we have a special treat for you tonight. Our favorite entertainer, Dale Hall, will be dancing authentic Eskimo dances with Olga and Oliver Amouak."

Lucy and I shifted around in our chairs trying to get the best view of the stage. We didn't want to miss a thing. There was a lot of music, jokes and nonsense before the dancing began. Dale finally came on stage with a beautiful Indian costume. She put on a great performance. After a break, Dale came back on stage and performed another dance, unique to another culture.

Lucy was anxious for her parents to come on stage.

"Maybe they'll be on for the grand finale," I whispered to her. Then Dale came into view wearing a black wig and the parky that Olga had made for the occasion. She was tall for an Eskimo, but in her special clothes, if her complexion had been darkened a bit, Dale looked Eskimo. Dale and Olga danced in perfect unison. Oliver was in his glory. He loved to perform. The audience applauded, whistled, and cheered enthusiastically. The dancers felt great, and so did Lucy and I.

We were about to leave when Lucy said, "Let's wait. I think there's more." We sat down and waited. The band played, and the announcer did a little more banter. The band stuck up a lively number.

"Ladies and gentlemen, your attention please! The time you've been waiting for has finally come, the grand finale of our great show tonight. None other than the beautiful, sensuous, exotic Dale Hall."

"Is that Dale?" Lucy asked curiously. "What is she going to do?"

"I think she's going to strip," I answered in amazement.

"No! Not Dale!" Lucy whimpered.

"I'm afraid so, Honey," I said, the reality sinking in.

There were a lot of wolf calls and whistles while Dale went through her routine. She had two large fans she waved from side to side, and front to back, as pieces of her flimsy attire magically drifted to the floor. But the big fans always managed to cover up the strategic areas. Lucy was breathless, but not nearly as taken back as Olga.

"How could she do such a dance in front of all these people?" Olga asked repeatedly.

I tried to explain that Dale was a professional dancer, and that it really wasn't a lot different from the other entertainment. Dale performed the last dance as professionally as any of the dances she had performed earlier without being vulgar. Of course, I viewed all this from a male perspective.

WORKING FOR ARC

The Fortymile River - Eagle

In the late 1940's, when the Eagle road was under construction, the Road Commission sent five of us to overhaul three Caterpillar tractors. The Fortymile River empties into the Yukon River 40 miles downstream from Dawson City, Canada. The town of Eagle is about 10 miles downstream from the Fortymile River. There was one Northern Commercial Company Store, a small library, and the town hall, which included a fire station, a mule barn with the mules' names over each manger, sled dog houses alongside the mule barn, a nice size warehouse and one officer's home. These last buildings were what was left of Fort Egbert. Eagle was a small town, probably just a dozen or more people.

We all had to find a place to stay. Two fellows had homes in Eagle and one of them offered one of the mechanics to stay with him. A friend offered me to use his cabin while in Eagle and the 5th man was offered a place to stay also. Only at the last minute, his friend had different plans for his cabin, so this man asked me if he could stay with me. I said sure.

This man was a little hard to work with on the tractors. He didn't want any help, so we didn't speak to each other while we were at work. But when we shared the cabin we got along just fine, sharing the chores, starting a fire in the stove, cutting wood, cooking a meal or whatever. I liked that.

This was a neat little cabin and there was only one book, <u>Gone with the Wind</u>. I started reading it when I came home for lunch. I could hardly put it down. I'd say to myself, *"Scarlet, if you don't behave yourself you will be out of this story soon."* I didn't realize that Eagle had a little library until it was about time for us to leave, so I didn't have a chance to take advantage of it.

There was a windmill to pump water for the community to share. The tower was enclosed all the way to the wind power device that pumped the water. One person was paid to keep the fire going and start it if it went out and somebody kept it supplied with wood.

There was an old timer living close to where I was living. I'd say good morning to him if he was outside. He asked me what my name was so I told him *Ray*.

He said, "I don't know what you look like, but I'll recognize your voice. I'm almost blind but I can still saw wood and walk to the water supply."

There was an elderly lady about the same age who was just about as blind as he was. She was also taking care of herself and still baking bread for sale to her neighbors. There was only one youngster in town, a 15 year old daughter of the store keeper.

Two or three days before we left, an old couple that were mining on the Fortymile river floated into Eagle about 3AM. Some time earlier, the husband had built a make-shift boat out of barrels cut in half length-wise and welded the sections together. He fastened some spruce poles on the sides and chinked the poles with rags to give it more freeboard. I assume he used this relic to cross the river once in a while. His wife had now had a stroke and was paralysed. To get his wife to Eagle safely, he placed a canvas over the top of his boat in case they shipped water. There are big rocks in that river and if you didn't have the skill to go past them you could upset your vessel.

Eagle is 300 or more miles as the crow flies from Fairbanks and flying weather was poor, so someone cared for her while they waited for a plane to arrive the next day. I heard she did OK.

Wiseman, Cat Repair

I was sent to the small village of Wiseman to work on a tractor in the spring. There were only a few people living there through the winter. The ARC usually sent one or two men to check the graders, the two short roads, and a Caterpillar (cat) trail and check out a cable that supported people to cross the river when the water was high. In the summer of 1948, the ARC decided to doze a trail on the north side of the river, the side the village is on with its nice 4000 foot airstrip. The airstrip would accommodate a large airplane like a DC 3 that landed shortly after I did with a cat-skinner named Axel, the man I would be working with. It was his job to operate the cat.

After the plane was unloaded and things settled, an old timer named Joe came over and told us we could use his old Chevy if we could get it started. We managed to start the old pickup and unloaded our supplies, lumber, and tool boxes.

After things were put away, except for our personal gear, Joe said, "Usually I rent this little cabin for a few dollars." Of course we both agreed it was a good deal. We carried our gear into the cabin and emptied our grub containers and fixed ourselves a little lunch. We just got started eating when Joe came in to ask us if we were going to the store.

"I could go," Joe said, "but I'm on the outs with the store keeper. It's been a while since we've seen eye to eye. A moose walked through town one day. I saw it and the store keeper saw it, and we both shot at it. I said I hit it and the store keeper said he hit it, and we haven't settled it yet. If you don't mind, take this note to him and tell that old @#$% he'd better give you my mail." That wasn't the only sore spot between them. Joe's wife Tissue was out with the dog team one day and the store keeper ran her off the trail. Joe sued the store keeper and won the case.

When I got back from the store with Joe's mail, he was pretty happy. He offered to loan me his rifle if I wanted a sheep. He said, "They come right in town sometimes." I could imagine how well that would go over with the local people, a total stranger shooting a sheep out of season! No thanks.

Axel and me walked over to the log shanty that belonged to the ARC. That little shack was so full of junk ... every nut and bolt and nail was saved for an emergency. It made sense, of course. It was at least 200 air miles to Fairbanks to the shop. Our equipment looked pretty good. We had a D7 Caterpillar, a three yard dump truck, 1931 vintage, and a pull grader. Joe had that old Chevy pickup and the store keeper had a Jeep. That's all the vehicles I saw in town. There was no doubt there was some equipment out on the creeks where the miners were working. Their equipment had to come up on a barge when the water was high enough. When we got the tractor or cat in good shape, we crossed the river where it was about 2 ½ feet deep and headed on the trail to the Stanish brothers who were mining 16 miles down stream.

We had no trouble going on the cat trail so we stopped to talk to an old fellow at Cold Foot. He was glad to have someone to talk to. It was the only cabin there before the haul road was built going to Prudhoe Bay. This old man said his wife worked for Charley Maine in Fairbanks.

Stanish Brothers

We drove up another couple of miles to reach Obrien Creek, where we shook hands with the old gold miners Sam and Brian Stanish who invited us for supper. To help them, we hauled a large load of wood close to their cabin to use for their slackline boiler. It was a small effort on our part for feeding us while we were there.

The Stanish brothers seem to get along very well. They had a nice garden and frozen moose meat cached in the frozen ground. An author had given them a book he had written and their names were mentioned in it. They could not read English but they knew where their names were.

These brothers worked their gold mine this way. I'll guess it was 12' to 16' to pay dirt. This was a winter phase of recovering gold in thawed ground. As winter approached they started digging six shafts about 5' square and about 4' apart. The resulting columns between the holes would freeze solid. As they dug down deeper these frozen columns became supports. That made it safe for the miner. They could lower a bucket into the shaft by way of the arrangement of cables called the slack-line, energized with a wood-fired steam engine, all the way down into the pay dirt. They'd fill the bucket and hoist it up to the surface and sluice it to separate the gold from the gravel in the spring. After all the pay dirt was hoisted out, they'd form a drainage field by placing rocks on the bottom of the void to serve as a drain pipe. That way, when the frozen columns thawed out they would fall to the exhausted pay dirt on the bottom and the home made pipe would keep the water continually running. These two men used this system for years for 500'.

Tractor Trouble

We started our project dozing a trail on the north side of the north fork of the Koyukuk River. We used the toilet paper system: I'd go ahead with a roll of toilet paper and hang a piece on a limb that Axel, the catskinner, could see from the cat. We hadn't gone over a 100' when the catskinner pushed a big spruce tree over, pulling the root system, which lifted the rear end of the cat up about 3' and letting the track hang slack. Axel wasn't paying attention. He kept trying to back it up. So the track came out of the sprocket and it wedged so tight into the inner housing we couldn't budge it.

We borrowed a house jack from the Stanish Brothers and tried lifting the track to get some slack so we could pound the track off the housing. No luck. We put heavy flat rocks under our house jack but we were just pressing the rocks further in the ground. We decided we'd take a pad off and then take a pin out of the track and pound it out. That didn't work either. We couldn't get the pin out.

The only thing left to do was to walk the 16 miles to Wiseman and call Fairbanks on the radio-type phone that was monitored once a day at a certain time. Brian Stanish was younger than Sam so he said he would go with us. The river was low so we walked on dry river bed. Brian was quite tall, 6'1" and a handsome rascal. His strong legs gave him a nice long stride.

As we walked to Wiseman, Brian told me the story about his sweetheart in the Old Country. When he was through he couldn't hold the tears back. It was a sad-sad story, which I wrote about in the poem "Where Love Lies." Tears come to my eyes almost every time I read it.

Problem Solving in the Wilderness

I reached Fairbanks on the radio phone and explained that I needed a cutting torch, new pat bolts and a new track link. Right after breakfast Axel and I started for Wiseman to get what we ordered. Halfway between Wiseman and the Stanish Brothers a small plane landed on the 2000' air strip that belonged to a mining group. There was a passenger in the plane, sent out to take my place.

Where Love Lies

I met an old man a few years back
living in a humble run-down shack.
He said he'd been on this creek 45 maybe 50 years.
A sad story it was, there were tears.

He told me that he left his sweetheart
when he was very young
to come to this great land,
planning to go back someday and ask for her hand.

The years kept rolling by.
Planting a garden, ahunting for moose,
grubbing for gold out of the ground.
Seems time for Sweetheart could not be found.

The idea was always in mind
that when that big bonanza he did find,
He would go back and make her his bride,
fulfill his promise, fulfill his pride.

It always seemed there was not enough.
There were things to buy, like grub and snuff.
Wood had to be cut and hauled.
No time for Sweetheart then, he bawled.

This is the story he told as he cried.
Too late for Sweetheart, for she had died.
Finally he realized he was very old.
He had no sweetheart, but lots of gold.

We talked to the equipment supervisor and the pilot. What we needed from Wiseman was a 6'2" piece of pipe and a ¾ inch heavy duty tool kit, a track wrench to loosen and a track tension spring and a track link to install. If there wasn't a cross wind, they could land and unload the parts from Fairbanks to the Stanish camp. We would walk back to the Stanish camp if the plane couldn't land because of the cross-wind.

The passenger Mr. Battersbee was tall and lean, 6'2" and about 175 pounds. I never heard his first name. We three decided to divide our load: a back pack of grub, some tools and a 6'2" pipe. We thought that would be the easiest for Mr. Battersbee to carry the pipe. We started walking down that beautiful airstrip till we got to the trees. Mr. Battersbee said "Let's stop. I can't go any further. I have a bum leg. If it gives out somebody will have to carry me."

I asked him if he could make it back to the camp. He said he would try. Once a day a Norseman (a short plane that will carry a ton or more) flew through there. If it landed, the pilot might be willing to take him to the town of Bettles and then he could fly to Fairbanks because a large plane landed there quite frequently. We left Battersbee and walked back to go to work on the tractor.

We slacked back the spring tension and tried cutting a track link with the little portable welding outfit. It didn't put out enough heat to cut off a link.

Ok. Another walk to Wiseman. I went by myself this time. I wanted to bring that 20 ton jack back with me from the ARC shack. I located it and looked around to see if there was anything else we could use. Then, I went to the cabin Axel and I rented.

To my surprise, Mr. Battersbee was there. I wondered why he didn't walk back on the foot trail. A plane didn't show up so he didn't know what to do.

"Let's have a little something to eat and then talk," I said. After we tapered off our appetites, Mr. Battersbee started to tell me a story, starting off with his home in California.

"That's where I owned two mortuaries that were very successful. My wife and I were well off financially and I take the blame for what broke up our marriage. I started drinking heavily and started complaining about my wife not taking good care of the house and other things. I was disgusted with her and she was disgusted with me. It's not very long ago when I thought life was over for me. I was drinking more than ever and I decided to buy a hand gun. I drew lots of money out of the bank and took the best car. I started driving north to find a place to pull off the road and shoot myself. The further I drove, the more my senses started to behave. After thinking about my wife and myself I decided to throw my weapon in the first river I crossed, and I did. I didn't know why I took so much money out of the bank and the best car if I was going to shoot myself. There must have been a message in the back of my head that said, 'Don't be a fool.' I'm sorry I went on and on with my story. I just had to talk with someone."

"I'm glad you did. I'm sure things are going to work out for you."

"Ray, what should I do while I'm here?"

"Well, the best thing I can think of is to go to work every morning at the Road Commission shack and try to organize all the nuts and bolts and anything else that could be improved. There is a grease gun and a can of grease. You can check the truck and the pull grader."

The next morning Joe came over to the cabin to ask me if I was going to walk back to OBrien Creek. I said, yes, I planned to.

Joe said, "I have a little inflatable boat I'll loan to you if you want."

"That sounds good, let me have a look at it." We unrolled it and pumped if full of air. It looked like a one man raft. My legs took most of the space. Mr. Battersbee took one look at it and said, "I'll never ride in that contraption!" so I just kept getting things ready so I could put the heavy hydraulic jack on the bottom. I had to gather some nice thin willow saplings to lay crossways and lengthways to support the heavy jack. There was no worry about tipping over or sinking. The biggest problem was not to damage the bottom on a sharp rock in shallow water.

At the last minute Mr. Battersbee came back to the cabin, took a second look at the raft and asked me if he could go with me. I said he could. I didn't know what changed his mind. Maybe he had never used a grease gun or changed oil in his life. We floated down the river just fine. When the river divided I just had to guess which side was the best. We had to get out a couple of times in shallow water so we didn't tear the bottom. The tractor track was like I left it.

I had a new idea. I checked if the Stanish Brothers had any hacksaw blades. They said they had five.

"Can I have them?" They both piped up, "Of course you can."

Even with the tension spring slack we couldn't budge the track between the sprocket and the gear housing. With the pad off I had room for the hacksaw to start sawing. The blades held up pretty well.

When the rail started to pinch the saw blade, I'd jack the rail up a bit to relieve the tension. All five blades were used up. I had sawed through about three-quarters of the track rail so I pumped the jack up and that broke the last part of the link. We had the whole business put together in 2 hours.

When I was packing my gear to leave, Brian Stanish asked me to come into his shed for a minute, saying "I have something to show you."

He pulled his gold pan off the shelf and told me to take a nugget. I hesitated. He said, "Help yourself. Take any one you want." I didn't want to be greedy so I took one abut the size of my middle finger nail. Gold was worth $35.00 an ounce then. The gold in his pan was worth quite a lot.

Radio

The road was under construction but all of it was not connected. Molly and Bob McComb were getting ready so they would be prepared to open their restaurant when the road was finished. Up to then the only way you could get to Chicken was by tractor, trail, foot trail or airplane. I must have been one of Molly's first customers. She asked me if I had my rifle along. I said no, I didn't.

"Well you had better take mine along because just about everybody has seen a huge bear roaming around."

I had about three miles to walk to Purdy's camp, a young family who were mining on Chicken Creek. I met Art Purdy on the cut he was working on and he said, "Come up to the house with me. We're going to listen to the Joe Louis fight in about 30 minutes. We'll help you with the tractor when the fight is over."

So I climbed up the hill to Art's cabin and met a couple of people I didn't know. Grandpa Purdy, Art's wife Agnes and Art's brother.

The boys had a comfortable place on the porch for Grandpa Purdy to sit with barrel tops on either side of him with the magic aroma drifting towards Grandpa from the smoldering powder. The little battery radio was pulling in sound waves about 260 miles away from Fairbanks, giving us the preliminaries of the big fight. Someone went down to the cellar and brought up with some homemade root beer.

The two fighters entered the ring. The referee introduced the boxers and the crowd went wild. The referee said, "Touch your gloves, fellows, and go in your corner and come out fighting."

We all got close to the radio except Grandpa. The two fighters started with a little sparring, feeling each other out and then suddenly Joe Louis charged in slugging with lefts and rights and knocked his opponent down. The referee made the count "1-2-3-4-5-6-7-8-9-10. You're out." It was all over in less than two minutes, and the referee raised Joe Louis's arm and declared him the World Champion. We were all stunned. None of us who were listening had even taken a sip of our root beer. I thanked my friends and said I'd better get back to work.

TRIP OUTSIDE ('52)

Fortymile Moose

My friend Bill Lefferson and I were chosen to go to the Fortymile River and straighten some Bridge steel that had fallen through the ice when crossing the river during the winter. We had been hunting moose the previous week and didn't have any luck, so we both took our rifles along just in case. We weren't too concerned if we were using a little Highway's time. We had 300 miles to drive. If we were late, which we would be, we didn't get paid over time anyway. Please don't get disgusted with me. I don't like to shoot animals. I raised my kids on moose, caribou and salmon. Since my last kid left home I haven't shot an animal. Hunting was not a sport to me.

We had a good time visiting and talking about prior hunts that we had been involved in. We turned off the Alaska Highway and drove about 20 miles. One of us thought we saw something that looked like a moose, standing close to some bushes, so we stopped the truck and looked through the binoculars. In those days, the law was you had to shoot a moose a ¼ mile off the road. Can you imagine trying to guess how far away an animal is? Not easy. Sure enough, we judged the moose was 450 to 500 yards away. It was a long shot. We shut the truck off and laid our rifles on the hood of the truck and fired. The moose went down.

Bill and I checked our truck for our butchering tools. As it turned, we didn't have any. Now that is dumb, just say it out loud. We had a moose that will dress out about 850 pounds. Bill located a hack saw and I had a Buck knife that had a blade that locked. We gutted the moose and started sawing it into pieces. We were about half done when a man walked through all the brush to visit us.

"Nice moose," he says.

"Yup," we both agreed.

"Be careful how you dress it out."

"Yup," we agreed.

"By the way fellows, do you have a hunting license?"

"Yup." "Can I see them?" We showed him our current licenses.

"Thank you fellows. Where were you boys when you shot the moose?" We both pointed to the truck.

"OK, boys, now take good care of that meat."

"Yes, sir. We will take good care of it." It's hard work carrying big pieces of meat to the truck, but we managed to carry all of it.

We were only about ten miles from Molly McCombs, the only place between Chicken and Eagle, and no bridge on the Fortymile River. Molly came out and asked us if we needed anything. We told her we were headed to the Fortymile, but we wondered if we could park our moose in that old barn. Molly said, "Sure. I'll get some rope for you."

Bill and I got the moose hung up and I asked her if she could send it to Tok on the first ARC truck to come through. They had a big walk-in freezer in one of the Alaska Highway buildings. That was where everyone stored their moose.

When Bill and I were hanging up our moose we noticed a big bear hide. I ask Molly if she knew who owned it. Molly said, "Sure. Are you interested in it?"

"If it's for sale and not too expensive, I'd like to buy it."

Bill and I went on our way to the Fortymile to start straightening and mending the bridge. About half of the steel was on the other side of the river. We had oxygen and acetylene tanks that were heavy so a trapper loaned us his canoe to transfer some of our gear across to the other side. Everything went well on our part of the project.

When we first got there, we carried the moose head up on top of the hill and laid it on what looked like a well worn bear trail. Well, it wasn't there in the morning. I learned later that the tongue was wonderful. So were the brains. I never left such wonderful food in the woods after that.

We headed back home and stopped to see Molly again. We saw our moose wasn't hanging up anymore. Molly said she sent it to Tok when a ARC truck came by. Molly also said the owner of the bear hide wanted $10 for it so I gave her the only money I had.

We stopped at Tok and picked up our moose meat and headed for Fairbanks. The weather was cool so we were able to keep our meat hanging outside.

Bear Rug

Old timers may recall how times were in Fairbanks, Alaska in 1951-1952. Life was not easy. Wages at the Alaska Road Commission (ARC) never seemed to stretch until the next payday, and the Northern Commercial Company owned us a good share of the time.

We lived in the college area and there were times that I walked the 4 ½ miles to work for lack of gas in my pickup. By 1951, Lucy and I had been married about four years and had two kids. Jerry was 2 ½ and Judy was a year old. Our house was very small, 20' square with one partition in the middle. Bad water was the reason we didn't want to expand our house. The water was horrid. We couldn't cook with it or wash clothes in it. It barely served to flush the toilet. We decided it would be better to relocate where there was better water and start over.

I did a dumb thing when I spotted that bear hide and asked Molly McComb if she would contact the owner of the hide to see if it was for sale. When I came back from working on the tractor, Molly said the owner would take $10 for it. "It's sold," I said, and gave her my last $10 'til pay day.

After I got home, I examined this hide, and I saw it wasn't that great. The light in the old barn where I bought it hadn't been very good and so I hadn't noticed all the defects. The hair on the belly was very thin, the moths had been in it, and little animals had been chewing on the edges. Lucy wasn't too happy with my "trophy."

Since I'd spent so much money on the bear hide, I wasn't going to let it go to waste. It was to have been my bear rug. There wasn't room for the hide in either room in the house, and so I put it in the doorway between the two rooms. Well! The hide wasn't tanned, so it didn't lay flat and we kept tripping on it. Lucy finally got disgusted with it and said it had to go.

"I'll fix it," I said. I cut the legs off and made a little rug. That didn't work either, so I finally threw it outside for an orphan dog to sleep on.

Ray and Lucy and the Cold War

We had made the decision to sell our house in the fall of '51 and move into my sauna on the adjoining lot. We sold our house for $17,000. Wow! What a pile of money. This was money to build our new house. We put it away in the bank for safe keeping so it wouldn't dribble away.

At the time we were in the Cold War with Russia. Fairbanks is just 600 miles from Russia as the Rayvin flies. ("Rayvin" is my nickname, from RAYnold IrVIN.) During required practice blackouts, a civil patrol checked the neighborhood to see if all the outdoor lights were out and all the windows well covered. That winter of living in our little sauna, we had half a moose hanging from a tree in the yard. I'd saw a hunk off before I went to work so Lucy could have something to prepare for supper.

Once in a while, I would tell Lucy, "Maybe I should take a little money out of our savings so I could fill the pickup tank."

"Nothing doing," Lucy would say. "That is our house money. Walk to work." She was right.

That $17,000 in the bank was beginning to burn our pockets. I saw two alternatives for our $17,000. One was to take all this money and buy material to build a new house. The other was to buy a new car and have one fine trip "Outside". With my maturity and sage judgment, I decided to do the sensible thing – buy the car and make the trip.

But when? We decided to go in April '52 for good road conditions. As winter set in, though, it seemed harder to cook with poor wood. The frozen moose got tougher to saw. We were tripping over my trophy bear rug, which I hadn't put outside yet. And I was walking to work several days a month. We started thinking, *Why wait till April? Why not go in March?*

I checked on buying a new car. Paul Greiman had just the car for us sitting in Seattle for only $5,000. We had $17,000.

What about this lousy water? Are we going to come back to this? No! We would find a lot in Slaterville. We heard they had pretty good water there. We managed to locate a lot and the owner would trade it for our old pickup. Things were shaping up. As the winter dragged on, our sauna seemed to be getting smaller and smaller.

"Is there much sense in waiting til March?" I asked Lucy. "With this Cold War thing going on with Russia, they might invade Alaska and we would never get to spend our money on a house!"

"What do you think of going the day after Christmas?" Lucy suggested, always ready to go. We decided that once we were in Seattle, we would buy a new outfit for each of us, and new suitcases, and travel in style in our new 1951 Plymouth station wagon.

Trip of '52

We got on the plane December 26. It was -40 below when we left Fairbanks. When we arrived in Seattle that Saturday evening it was raining. We checked into the same hotel that all the old-time Alaskans stayed in when they went to Seattle. We were all too warm in our Alaskan winter clothing, so we decided to shop for our new outfits. We didn't realize all the shops were already closed for the weekend, so we had to make the best of it. We looked like idiots walking around in such warm clothing in the rain. My beaver skin hat started to get curly. I took it off (and got a heck of a cold).

The kids were fussy. We didn't have canned milk and they wouldn't drink fresh milk. A waitress told us we could find some at a little delicatessen down the street. We located the little store and bought the milk and then we retired to our room. The kids went to sleep as content as a couple of little bear cubs. I laid there awake awhile, wondering how we'd get out of the 7th floor in case of a fire.

After waiting four days for the dealer to prepare our new car for us, we got our beautiful gray 1951 Plymouth station wagon. Then we were on our way for what would be a wonderful trip, following the Pacific Coast Highway through the big redwood trees, staying in fine motels and eating great meals. Yes, siree! We were living it up first class. We kept a little supply of grub to cook in the motels and a supply of canned milk for the kids. Judy did squash a dozen eggs on the rear seat cushion, but that was the only blemish to the trip as we went south. It was a grand trip. We went all the way to Mexico. They thought my little Eskimo Lucy was Mexican. We bought souvenirs, had our pictures taken next to a burro, ate Mexican food. We traveled east from there to Texas and then north to Minnesota to visit my relatives and introduce Lucy to them.

We visited as many relatives as I could find in Minneapolis. We went to Duluth, where Jerry got a high fever and then small pox. He was miserable, itching and trying not to scratch. We took him to a doctor, who said Jerry would be sick for two weeks and that a week after Jerry would get well, and then Judy would get smallpox too. Jerry was well in two week, so we decided to visit Duluth before Judy came down with it. Just a day after our return to Minneapolis from Duluth, Judy came down with small pox. These childhood illnesses tied us up for five weeks. Our money was dwindling away.

It was March, and we had to think of heading home. Lucy added up our money. We had just a little over $300 left. *"That will be enough,"* I thought. All travelers were supposed to have a minimum of $300 to cross the U.S. border into Canada. Canada didn't want to have travelers become stranded.

We had that $300 when we left Bloomington, Minnesota, but we didn't have $300 when we got to the border. The customs man asked us how much money we had.

"About $300."

"Can I see it?" I pulled out my wallet and laid all the money out so the customs man could see it. There was only about $260. I turned to Lucy and told her, "Get the traveler's checks from the car."

She almost said, "What travelers checks?" But by the look on my face, she knew it was a charade.

"O.K." she said.

The customs man said "Never mind, be on your way. Have a nice trip." And he waved us on.

March was supposed to be the best time to travel the Alaska Highway. There was only about eighty miles of blacktop out of Edmonton, and gravel the next 2,000 miles to Fairbanks after that. The gravel was usually frozen and there was very little dust to contend with. Winter travel was usually the best as far as road surface was concerned if you didn't encounter extremely cold or slippery weather.

Everything went fine 'til we got somewhere between Grand Prairie, Alberta and Dawson Creek, British Columbia. A "Chinook" that affected about a 30 mile section of the road descended, leaving mud about 8" deep to drive through. Every time a vehicle passed us we had to stop and clean the windshield. I wasn't prepared. All we had was a box of Kleenex. The mud was too deep to step out of the car, so each time I had to open my door and try to reach as far as I could on the driver's side. Luckily there wasn't a lot of traffic, so I could go three or four miles between cleanings.

One time, though, I saw a Jeep approaching us way up the road while I was cleaning the windshield. I tried to hurry and get it cleaned and get the door shut before he got too close. Apparently the driver of the Jeep had seen me cleaning my window and thought he'd have a little fun. He headed straight for our car. When he got within 30' of us, he cut suddenly to the right so he skidded broadside to us and really covered our car with about ½ inch of mud. I wanted to turn around and run him down. But I had second thoughts. I didn't think I could catch him and it wouldn't have accomplished anything anyway. He might have been a 6'4" giant. Besides, Lucy didn't want me to.

After we got through the mud, we hit cold air again and all the mud froze to the car. We couldn't roll the windows down, and we had to pound on the doors to get them open. There was lots of snow that winter, so the berms were high along the side of the road. It was impossible to park off the road. There weren't any houses, so it wasn't easy to judge where to stop for the night. Two nights in a row we had to sleep in the car. The kids were bundled up in a sleeping bag in the rear of the car on top of our new sewing machine and other things we had bought, and we covered up in the front seat the best way we could.

During one of our nights parked along the berm, Lucy and I got cold and woke up about 3:30 AM. I started the car to warm it up and then decided to start traveling till we found a roadhouse open. We drove along for about three hours. I spotted a light and then saw a makeshift roadhouse sign.

"Let's go over there. I think I saw a light," I told Lucy. When we drove in the yard, we could see they were doing their best to get their new business established. The building was plenty rustic, constructed from the local trees, and building material was poking out of the snow everywhere, giving us the impression that the owners had just got the building habitable as winter closed in. There were several barrels of fuel scattered helter-skelter and a barrel pump was in one of them. We needed gas and I was hoping the barrels were clean. If there was water in them, it was surely frozen.

When we drove into the driveway, the light I had seen disappeared, so we just parked there a few minutes wondering if we had really seen a light. I was just about ready to turn around and leave when a lady holding a lantern opened the door and motioned us to come in. It was warm and cozy in the cabin, with the aroma of freshly split spruce and a gentle whiff of wood smoke. The lady asked us if we wanted breakfast.

"Anything you have would be fine."

"How about hot cakes, bacon and eggs?"

The lady then told us there was a bucket of water in a little side alcove and hot water was on the stove if we wanted to wash up. We could hear the sizzle of the bacon and smell the tantalizing aroma drifting our way. Oh boy! This was just like home. After we cleaned up, we sat down to a hearty breakfast, family style with extra food on a platter for a second helping. That humble log cabin was the nicest place we stopped on the whole trip. The lady gave me a measuring can so I would know how much gas I pumped in the car. We paid her and we were on our way again.

There were very few vehicles traveling the highway so we got to recognize many of them as they passed or when we met them at a gas stop. One car in particular had our attention. It was a beautiful, new, green Oldsmobile. These people were driving faster then we were but they stopped more often. Many times after they made a stop they would pass us. If it was narrow I'd slow down so they could get around me easily. It finally got to the point where they would toot their horn and wave and we'd do the same thing in return.

I told Lucy I didn't care what time we got to Whitehorse, we were going to stop and rest and take a bath. We arrived there about 2 PM. There wasn't a lot of choice besides the Whitehorse Inn for lodging, but we weren't particular. All we needed was a good sleep.

The first place we came to looked relatively new and inviting. When we checked in, we were given a key and a room number and were told where the wash house was. There wasn't any heat in the room but there was a nice air-tight wood stove and a box full of dry wood. It wasn't long before the small room was cozy as could be. I told Lucy that while she and the kids took a bath, I'd go see if I could get the car washed. I drove down the street two or three blocks and spotted a gas station.

The attendant said, "Wow! You sure need a wash! Where did that mud come from?" I told him the story, and he said that if I left the car there, he'd have his wash boy get on it as soon as he got back. The attendant then said to me, "Let me show you something before you leave."

I followed him into the work stalls, and there I saw a 1951 Plymouth station wagon just like ours, But the cab was sheered off just above the hood clear to the rear seat. A big flatbed truck had slid off the road on a curve. This car slid off on the same curve and went right under the extended flatbed, killing the driver instantly. The car was loaded with supplies, including a case of eggs that were smashed all over the interior. The horrible sight gave me the shivers. It could have been us.

Just as I was leaving, I saw the green Oldsmobile we had met so many times pull into the station. I waited a minute or so till he came to a stop and then I said, " Howdy, neighbor. Gee! Your car is all polished up. Where did you get the wash job done?"

With a disgusted look, he said "At Dawson Creek. I wish I had never stopped there. Take a look at my hood." He had left his car at a station to be washed while he and his wife went to eat lunch. When they returned to pick up their car they looked in disbelief at the hood of their car. The young fellow that washed it had climbed up on the hood wearing heavy work shoes to wash the top, putting some scratches and dents on the hood of his beautiful new car.

Lucy and the kids already had their showers and the kids were snuggled in bed when I got back to the hotel. Lucy said there was lots of wonderful hot water for a shower. I told Lucy about the car like ours. She gasped at the thought of what could have happened to us.

We got ourselves a nice rest and we were getting very anxious to head for Fairbanks the next day. The mild weather had made the road very slippery. We drove very cautiously with the thought in our minds of what could happen. We hadn't driven very many miles north of Whitehorse when we came to the curve where the car had slid under the flatbed. The truck was still there. I slowed down and was extra careful all the way to Fairbanks.

We arrived in Fairbanks, happy to be home in familiar surroundings and reunited with our family. On the other hand, I could see us scratching to get ourselves established again. Of the $17,000 from the sale of our house, after our trip and purchases outside we arrived in Fairbanks with $100.

We were back in our little sauna stoking our little cookstove, making plans for the future. It did cross our minds that maybe we did a foolish thing. But as time went on, we had no regrets.

We moved our sauna to Slaterville onto the lot we traded for the pickup and our family increased with three more kids: John, Jewel and June. It would be twenty years before we were able to make a trip "Outside" again. The Trip of '52 was one of the most rewarding trips we ever made, but I wouldn't have done the same thing 20 years later.

JACK WADE CREEK

Tractor Repair

The Alaska Road Commission was just in the process of surveying the road to Eagle. It is upstream from Eagle that the Fortymile river empties into the Yukon River. The spot is forty miles downstream from Dawson City Yukon Territory, Canada. At the beginning of the surveying process, the proposed road didn't have a name yet. It would become Taylor Highway, but I still call it the Fortymile or Eagle road. (One of my neices is named Taylor after that road). The new road would take off from the Alaska Highway somewhere close to Mile Post 1300.

I was told to go to Jack Wade Creek to work on a tractor. They were sending me there to install a new timing gear for a D-4 tractor. Jack Wade is roughly 70 miles from Eagle. The only way to get to Jack Wade Creek during the survey was by air, tractor, or foot. I got my gear together, some canvas for shelter over the tractor, my tent, grub for my belly, and tools. A caterpillar manual was given to me to take along for reference.

I'd been waiting at the airport for the plane to land for quite awhile. It was a Norseman and had the letters on the side, "Paul Bunyon" Minnesota Air Service. The pilot was testing it because it had just arrived from Minnesota the day before. The mechanics changed the propeller and asked the pilot to give it another try. There was still something wrong. So the mechanics did something else; I don't know what. But the pilot said it was better, so he told me to gather my gear and put it in the plane.

We headed toward Big Delta, 100 miles SE of Fairbanks, following the road all the way, and then he turned south east for about 30 or 40 miles, and then he turned back towards Big Delta again.

"It still doesn't sound right," the pilot said.

He landed on the military side of the airstrip at Ft. Greeley. An officer came running out of his office and shouted, "You can't leave it here. Park it over by the FAA space."

"Yes, sir. If it will start."

Fort Greely is only about five miles from Delta, but there wasn't any local transportation. We must have bummed a ride to the Triangle Cafe, located right in the triangle where the information center is today, at the official end of the Alaska Highway.

"We just as well have lunch while we're here," the pilot said.

"I'm not hungry," I said. "I'll just have a cup of coffee." While I was wiaiting for my coffee, though, I noticed a sign on the bulletin board that said "ARC people sign here," giving me credit against my pay.

"By George, I think I'll have a bite to eat after all," I said.

When we got back to Fort Greely, the pilot got in touch with the FAA manager and asked him if he could contact a plane coming our way. A plane would be landing in a few minutes.

"You can transfer you cargo and your passenger to the Robin," he said.

There were two airstrips, one in the valley at Jack Wade Creek and the other one high on a hill at Boundary where there were just a couple of cabins. Between the airstips was a road which, since the road was constructed, is now called Top of the World Highway. It was

Alaska, No Regrets

about 12 miles from Jack Wade. Keep going and you would wind up at the Yukon River.

There are strong crosswinds at Top of the World road, so we landed at Jack Wade. We could see a truck coming down to get his freight. I unloaded my gear. My tractor manual was missing. *"Holy Smokers! What will I do now? By guess and by gosh I'll have to figure it out someway,"* I thought. All the parts were with me, including the fiber gear. I set up my canvas shelter because it started raining. Then I took a good look at the tractor to see how I was going to approach this rascal.

I had had a little time to look at the manual when the mechanics were getting the Norseman checked out, so I wasn't completely in the dark. I finally got into the innards and I could see what lay ahead. The fiber gear had many teeth stripped off. That meant there were lots of broken pieces in the oil pan. I pulled the gear off and checked the one I had brought with me against it. They matched. I knew that I'd have to drop the oil pan and dump the oil out and clean the residue out.

Gold Miners Help

One of the gold miners came over to see what I was doing.

"If you need any help, just speak up. We have a good supply of cat parts," he said. I explained what I was doing and told him what I needed was a few quarts of motor oil for the crank-case and gasoline for the starting engine.

"I'll show you where the oil is and my wife has a gallon of gasoline for her washing machine that you can have. She has more. My wife invites you for supper tonight. She will be ready in a couple of hours." I walked with him to get the crankcase oil and carried what I could back to the cat. I would bring the gasoline when I came back from supper.

I put the fresh oil in the tent and did a few other things I had to do. A caribou came down from the hills to see what I was doing. He was only about 20 feet away from the tractor. Caribou are very curious, and there are times when it is their downfall, because they can be easily shot.

Up at the cabin, I was introduced to the people I hadn't met yet. They were young folks. One of the ladies had a two year old and was due to have another child.

"Do you plan to name the new baby *Jack Wade* if it's a boy?"

"No. We have already discussed this subject. We have 2 or 3 names in mind already."

"Maybe my wife and I were too hasty to name our kids," I said. "I would have like to have named my daughters, *Kluane, Tundra Rose*, and *Alaska*. (My daughters Judy, Jewel, and June tell me they are glad I didn't name them any of those names. Their mother's father gave all of my kids Eskimo names: *Deegigalook, Ganiduk, Buningjung, Lapsin*, and *Ahkowak*.)

I offered to pay these young folk for what they gave, but he said, "I have a better idea. Talk to the Fairbanks district engineer Frank Nash and ask if we can stay in the ARC camp this winter for a day or two. How does that sound?" These folks were hauling supplies in for the summer mining season. They would only stay a day or two.

"Sounds great! I'm sure Frank will give you permission. Thank you for the lovely meal." Since it was time for me to leave, I also asked if they could direct me to where the survey crew was working.

"See that trail going straight up that hill? That's where their camp was located, but I'm not sure if they will still be there. There was some question if the road was going to be located on top of the hill or down here in the valley. The only thing I can tell you is there is an old cat trail on your right that goes to a place called Franklin, an old mining camp that is abandoned."

Reaching the ARC Crew

I worked a couple more days and finished my tractor repair and then the next day I headed the direction I was given. I found a couple of empty barrels and remnants of a fireplace. I set my tent up and built a fire for company. It was already dark. I didn't have any candles or flashlight. Besides, I didn't have anything to read, either.

I was tired, but I wasn't sleepy. I had my mosquito net set up inside my tent. It was OK for awhile until I got too warm and the mosquitoes were getting in someplace. I slept a little now and then and tossed around till 3:00 A.M. when the sun was coming out. I put my clothes on and went outside and discovered the mosquitoes were horrendous. I walked around for a couple of hours to see if I could find the trail I was looking for.

I had some ideas where I should go. I came in contact with the Franklin trail. It was very visible and that encouraged me, because I had a starting point. There were many tracks in the moss, but it was a guide anyway, so I went back to my camp to get the tractor and my belongings.

I don't know how far I drove, ten miles or more. I could tell by the changes in the terrain that I was approaching the Fortymile River. Ahead of me was a dozed trail on top of a ridge.

I had been going slowly up and down over these ridges but this one I had come to was a real steep one. This hill sloped down several hundred feet on both sides. Without having the weight of a dozer blade on the front, my tracks started scratching the gravel and the front end started bucking backwards. I slide off the seat. I grabbed the fuel tank on the right side of the tractor and pulled myself back onto the seat. I grabbed the steering levers, put my feet on the brakes, and took it out of gear. I just sat there for a minute or two and then let the tractor roll back in the saddle of this ridge. I wasn't sure if my pants were just wet or if something more embarrassing had happened. I threw my sleeping bag and Trapper Nelson Pack board, with which I could carry all I needed, off the tractor and hoofed it down towards the river. When I got there, I met the leadman.

"Where's the tractor?" he asked.

"It's up on the ridge. I just scared the life out of me. I almost fell off the tractor. I'll go up there and get it in the morning."

The survey crew was setting up a camp on a nice level place by the river. It had been a steady rain for several days. I was so dirty I wanted to take a bath in the river, so I stripped off my cloths and jumped in. The water was so cold I couldn't stay in very long. One of the guys called, "How's the water, Ray?"

"It's fine! Come on in!"

He jumped in: "Wow! Wow! I thought you said it was warm!"

"No, I said it was fine."

I wasn't in the river long. When I was ready to get out, I went to the rock where I had laid my soap. It was gone. It seemed to me the river was rising and had floated my soap away. I jammed a stick into the gravel so that we could pay attention to the river rising. It was coming up a foot an hour.

We ate supper that evening and watched our water marker. The water was already in the tents a couple of inches and it continued to rise. Finally the leadman said we had better take our personal gear up the hill and plan on sleeping up there. He said the cook would have to make our breakfast on a camp fire. Every one of us took the leadman's advice, except one man.

"I'm not moving out till the water's within one inch of my sleeping bag," he said. About midnight, he had his arms full of his gear and was stumbling through the brush and rocks. He had his flashlight in his mouth, because he didn't have enough hands to hold everything.

The next day, the leadman told one of the guys to take me with him to Jack Wade because a plane would be there with supplies for the camp. The guys found an old horse-drawn wagon to pull with the tractor. It was much better than dragging a go-devil if you didn't stick a leg into one of the big wheel spokes. We weren't there long when the plane arrived and I was on my way home again to be with Lucy and my kids.

The Gold Dredge

It was decided that that section of the new road should go in the valley of Jack Wade Creek. There's an old gold dredge located there, kind of wedged in between the creek and the road. This dredge must have been moved there a few years after the Klondike Gold Rush at Dawson City. It would be interesting to know the history of that old relic. I can only imagine that the dredge was moved there piece by piece. The dredge parts must have been barged from Seattle to the Yukon River all the way to Eagle. From Eagle, the parts would have had to have been hauled by horses to Jack Wade Creek, about 70 miles, and then to have been assembled there. Gold must have been worth around $22 an ounce in those early days. It was only worth $35 in the 1940's.

UNCLE BILLY, EARTHQUAKE (1960'S)

Uncle Billy

Uncle Billy was born in Unalakleet, on the lower Yukon River in Alaska, in about 1875. Uncle Billy was twenty-two years older than his brother, my father-in-law Oliver Amouak. I never saw Uncle Billy read anything. He was raised the old way, pretty much a subsistence life. His education in how to survive was acquired from his elders. Uncle Billy was tall for an Eskimo. Even at 80 he was 6' tall.

(Oliver had gone to school up to Second grade. My mother-in-law Olga didn't have a formal schooling. Everything she learned was from an older sister who had a disabled arm. Olga didn't know her mother's name; apparently she must have died when Olga was born.)

After Uncle Billy's wife died, he moved to Fairbanks from Fortuna Ledge on the Yukon River in about 1961. Uncle Billy stayed with Olga and Oliver for a few months in Fairbanks, but he didn't seem to be very happy. He was treated well, but he was bored stiff. There wasn't anything for him to do. Oliver would say, "Be careful of your heart."

Lucy and I wondered if Uncle Billy would like to stay with us in Delta. Lucy asked Uncle Billy if he would like to move to Delta, and he agreed to give it a try. Uncle Billy adapted to our home very well. He wasn't a burden to anyone. He was independent and resourceful.

He mended his own clothing and didn't expect anyone to wait on him. The only thing he let Lucy do was his wash.

Moose Hunting with Uncle Billy

We went moose hunting together up the Tanana River and the Goodpasture, a tributary to the Tanana. We started upstream with my 19' square stern Grumman canoe. We allowed ourselves 4 gallons of gas for my 7 HP motor. Uncle Billy was my pilot, reading the weather, pointing left or right so I would miss a gravel bar or obstruction. We would stop wherever we thought there was a big meadow or swamp to look for a moose.

A few miles up the Goodpasture, we came to a large opening, so we beached the canoe and secured it tightly to a tree. Deciding to camp for the night, Uncle Billy started preparing camp while I examined the big clearing. I walked about ¾ of a mile and spotted a large moose. I shot it and went back to the river to get Uncle Billy to help me. We dressed it out, skinned it, and cut it in nine pieces and spread it out on some brush we gathered in order to keep the warm meat off the ground. In late August, the days are still fairly long, so we had plenty of time to set up camp and cook supper. We were jubilant. We would eat well this winter!

The next morning the big job was waiting for us: packing the mooose to the river. Uncle Billy prepared a network of willow, so the canoe could be ready for us to lay the meat on. I started with the rib cage, one half of the front quarter. It weighed about 200 lbs. While I was lashing the rib cage to my pack board, Uncle Billy loaded a pack sack with the liver, heart, tongue, brains and leaf lard. It was a heavy load. I told Uncle Billy he didn't have to pack anything out, but he insisted.

Uncle Billy got to the canoe before I did. The canoe deck was nice and clean, so we didn't get sand and dirt on the meat and it had plenty of air. The other pieces were too heavy for Uncle Billy, so he packed our camp gear and kept the fire going for my coffee breaks after each round trip.

While we were close to the river, a boat pulled up to see how we were doing. It was lucky he stopped. I wanted to send word to Lucy who had been expecting me back the day before. I said to the boater, "If you see a gray Plymouth with five kids in it at the bridge, that's my wife. Would you tell her we will make it to the bridge tonight?"

He said, "Sure enough! Take good care of the meat."

While we were having coffee, I heard a moose crossing the river upstream from us and I wanted to see if I could call him just for fun. I didn't want to shoot him, because we didn't need more meat. He was grunting *ugh-ugh-ugh*, so I walked in the direction I heard the moose and concealed myself in the brush. Uncle Billy's hearing was so bad that he couldn't hear himself banging around the Grumman. I tried to get his attention to tell him to be quiet, but he didn't see me. I tried calling the moose. I waited a few minutes and called again and waited. I decided he didn't hear me, so I started walking back to the canoe. Then the brush and trees started cracking and stirring. The moose was about to investigate me. I dove into the brush myself and waited. In about 45 seconds, he stopped about 30' from me, wondering where I was and who I was. I let him stand there for about 30 seconds or so and stood up. When he decided I wasn't a moose, he took off.

We finished loading the canoe and decided if we were lucky we could make it to the bridge before dark. Our canoe was designed to carry 1,500 pounds. I think we maxed out. (I weighed our moose after it hung for 2 weeks. The forequarters and the neck dressed out over 1,000 pounds.) Besides the moose and us, we carried our camping gear, the kicker, fuel, lift, and moose hide of about 80 pounds. I had about 2 gallons of fuel left. We worked the canoe off the sand and shoved off down stream. We had about 2" freeboard. I started the kicker, but the square stern went lower than the surface of the river, so I quickly shut it off.

We started paddling downstream. Now, I'm not a white water canoe man, so I'm not about to try any fancy stuff. Maneuvering that heavy a canoe load is like trying to maneuver a submerged log. Pick your course way ahead of time, play it safe.

It started to get dark. Being that Alaska's twilight is so long, I figured we would make it to the bridge before it got dangerous. Everything was going well. We saw a float plane flying towards us about 20' above the water. He landed close enough to us that we could hear him speak above the drone of his engine. He kept his speed just right so he would drift downstream as fast as we were.

"Do you fellows need help? Your wife is worried about you."

"No, we're OK. Thanks"

"How about the old timer? Do you want me to take him to the bridge?"

"No. He's OK. I need his help. We'll be there in an hour or so. Thanks." He took off.

It was dark enough now that it was hard to tell if a log was floating by or if there was a canoe off at a distance. When we got to the landing, there was no little wifey waiting for me. I wanted her to see our moose that I was so proud of. But she had waited so long the night before she didn't think we would make it this night either.

Donnelly Dome and Lucy's Land

We spent much time at Donnelly Dome, a lonely deposit of glacial moraine about a thousand feet above the road and about 20 miles from Delta Junction, because Lucy claimed 160 acres for her Native land allotment. Her land is located across the road from Donnelly Dome, which was named after a prospector. It has a view of Donnelly Dome. From Lucy's land you can also see a mountain range facing southeast called the Granite mountains. Facing west you're looking at the Alaska Range, where the oil pipeline is about a mile away. I saw a moose on top of the Dome one time.

Uncle Billy wanted to go hunting at Donnelly Dome for parki squirrels or *siksikpuk* for Olga to use to create a parki. We got some camping gear and I loaned Billy my 300 Savage. The next day after his tent was set up, a 90 mile wind stirred up his camp. He had to put a ring of heavy stones around his tent. We went to Donnelly Dome to check on Uncle Billy in the middle of the week.

"How are things going, Billy?"

"Fine. Just fine," he said. "I shot a few squirrels and I have a few Sailor Boy Crackers left."

Helicopter Search for Uncle Billy and Jerry

Uncle Billy wanted to go moose hunting again next hunting season. Lucy and I were apprehensive about him going off by himself. His heart wasn't perfect. Jerry, our oldest son, was about twelve. He wanted to go too. We didn't want Uncle to go by himself, so we decided they should go together.

Uncle Billy climbed to the top of the Dome to look the country over. This must have been the best place to look for game during the old bow and arrow days. The Salcha Indians called it Moose Hill. We hauled Uncle Bill and Jerry to Donnelly Dome. Uncle pointed toward the head of Jarvis Creek.

I said, "OK, Uncle. We'll pick you and Jerry up Friday evening and I'll hunt with you on the weekend." I told Jerry to use Donnelly

Dome for his landmark. "Don't just follow Uncle Billy. Pick out dependable landmarks as you go. You might have to come back by yourself."

Jerry got a little excited. "Why should I have to come back alone?"

"You might get a moose and have to come and get me for help."

The real reason I wanted him to be sure he could get back by himself was that we thought Uncle Billy might have a heart attack. I was hoping they DIDN'T shoot a moose a long way from the road. I did have an old military vehicle to retrieve a moose if it was necessary.

On Friday when I got off work, Lucy and I went to pick up the hunters. There wasn't a sign of them anywhere. We hung around till it really got dark. I told Lucy that if they got a moose on the way back to camp, they could not possibly make it back, so we went home.

Saturday morning we went to the Dome again. It was snowing hard. You couldn't see the Dome from the road. Now we got worried. We hung around and examined their camp. Uncle Billy had bundled up their gear and tied it on some brush off the ground so it wouldn't get wet. We opened the cache and discovered Jerry's warm jacket in the bundle. *"Oh, my God! He's freezing!"*

It was dark again, so we stopped at the state troopers' office to report the missing men. There was an Army Military Police in the office listening to what we were saying.

"Pardon me, sir. I may be able to help. We have two soldiers marooned across the Delta River that we have to rescue with our helicopter in the moring. We'll be flying right over this area you described. When we're through with our mission we will look for you."

"Thank you, sir. We'll be there." I described the color of the parkis we would be wearing.

We couldn't sleep. At 2:00 a.m. we got up and made some coffee, filled the thermos and prepared to leave. We were at Donnelly Dome long before we could see to walk any place.

I had an idea. When I was scouting earlier, we camped on a nice creek called Ober Creek, with lots of dry wood and good clear water. I told Uncle Billy one time when we were exploring that Ober Creek would be a great place to camp when we went hunting. Uncle Billy agreed. I knew they planned to go many miles beyond this creek, but maybe on their way back Uncle Billy might think of it.

It had snowed about 8" and it was wet, heavy snow. We didn't think the chopper would make it. We couldn't see the Dome or anything else. We walked to Ober Creek, about 2 miles off the road. We were soaking wet by the time we got there. We were so wet we just walked back and forth across the creek, not aware that we were getting any wetter. I fired my rifle every once in a while, hoping I would hear rifle fire in return. It never happened.

We saw something red and fresh wolf tracks ahead of us. I wondered if the red was blood.

Finally about 10:00 a.m. we could hear the helicopter's *clattery-clattery*, but we couldn't see it. The chopper was going past Donnelly Dome to make their first rescue. An hour later the chopper circled over us and landed. It was the largest single prop I'd ever seen. A crew member stepped out of the chopper and invited us in. There were 6 or 7 people in it. The noise was so bad we had to shout in each other's ears. The soldier asked me if I had any ideas. I suggested that we make small circles and head upstream of this creek. We were not in the air 10 minutes when I saw a single plume of smoke rising straight up without a puff of air to disturb it. I said to myself, *"God, that has to be them."*

The helicopter landed close to the camp. Jerry and Uncle Billy ran up to the chopper. Uncle Billy said, "What's the matter?" Jerry had on a flimsy jacket and Uncle Billy had an abessed tooth that had swollen his cheek and closed one eye. Needless to say, we were so grateful for the army's help to find them. Uncle Billy told me they had trouble starting the fire we saw – everything was so wet.

The soldier asked, "Should we wait till they break camp?"

"No," I said. "I'll help them pack out, but if you don't mind taking my wife to the car I would appreciate it."

The chopper got up about 50' before I felt the car keys in my pocket. The soldiers dropped Lucy off at the car. A pickup came by. They saw Lucy standing by the car and picked her up and took her to Delta. She was so wet she would have really gotten cold waiting for us. It was a happy ending.

Uncle Billy's Master's Degree in Wilderness

Uncle Billy was always busy making things for us. He made me a pair of snow shoes with birch frames and strung with *bibish* (rawhide) from a mooseskin I had. He made model dogsleds and a canoe. And he made a real working dog sled.

Uncle Billy asked me if I knew where there was a good stand of birch. I did, and I took him out there. He carefully looked them over and picked one out. "This one will do," so I cut it down.

Uncle Billy rigged up a jig between two trees vertically and rip sawed all his boards for the sled. I had a 5 FF crosscut saw, not a ripsaw, but he just kept sawing until he had a bunch of thin 8' boards. I told him to use my tools. "Ja, ja," he said, but he made himself a bow drill and bits from nails.

He cut all the *bibish* from my moosehide for lashing the sled together. He bought a few small bolts to bolt the deck down. I asked him if he was going to put steel strips on the runners. "Ja, ja."

"I'll get you some strap iron when I go to Fairbanks. I'll make you a steamer to bend the wood," I offered. "Ja, ja." But before I knew it Uncle Billy had the wood bent and the steel on the runners.

"How did you bend the wood?"

"I took this old barrel to the river and cut the top off with your hacksaw and filled it two-thirds with water and built a fire under it and cooked the wood and bent it."

"How about the steel on the runners?

"I cut strips of the same barrel with your hacksaw." It was a beauty.

Uncle Billy got his Master's degree in the wilderness. Uncle Billy's wife had always said she never knew if she would see him again when he took off in the spring. In the fall Uncle Billy had always taken his sled and dogs to trap. I don't know how often he came home from the trap line, but I would imagine every time he made a round trip. But it was different in the spring. When he was trapping muskrats he would stay as long as he could 'til the ice went out and he would come home on the river. He would build a canoe around his sled. He took canvas and whatever else he needed to build the canoe around his sled and his dogs would run along the beach and follow him home.

Uncle Billy could read the weather by looking up at the sky in the evening. He could read the water in a stream. I learned quite a bit about reading water from watching Uncle Billy. I'm sure there are many more things I would have learned following Uncle Billy around. It was an education to be out in the wilderness with Uncle Billy, and also with my father-in-law Oliver Amouak.

Uncle Billy was hired to bring a plane that had an accident up river from their village. I don't know all the details of the rescue, but he built a raft and floated the plane to where he lived.

If Uncle Billy had told me he was going to walk to Nome from Fairbanks, he would have made it. He would take a good light axe, his rifle, ammunition, a light cup (birchbark in a pinch), spoon or homemade chopsticks, light tent, light canvas, change of clothes, his best skinning knife, light tin frying pan, salt and pepper. Uncle Billy would live on berries, caribou and squirrels. He could follow the "serum trial" from Nenana to Nome if he wanted to. Uncle Billy was part of the wild land.

1964 Anchorage Earthquake

Earthquakes in Fairbanks were not uncommon.Every once in a while one would shake the flexible bridge and knock some merchandise on the floor. We were living in Delta Junction, 100 miles Southeast of Fairbank, during the Anchorage Eathquake on Good Friday, 1964.

We were playing pinochle with Lucy's sister Pauline. We heard a rumble and felt a shake or two, but didn't think much of it until the house started shaking really hard. I yelled out loudly, "Let's get out of here!" and ran outside. Nothing was damaged that I know of except our well water was muddied.

Four days after the earthquake, we went to Anchorage to see if Lucy's cousins were OK because we didn't have a telly and Anchorage radio waves didn't come in clear to Delta. The first place we went to was to visit an elderly cousin that worked as a baker in the Native hospital. We invited her to go with us on a tour. We drove as close as we were able to and walked the rest of the way.

We were shocked at the amount of damage in Anchorage. Fourth and Fifth Avenues were a mess. Sections of the street on Fifth Avenue dropped several feet, and many buildings were damaged. On Fourth Avenue, sections of cement and stone from the Penny's store dropped onto the sidewalk and street. A big tall building about thirteen stories high was cracked between every window. This tall building had their radio station on the top, scaring the wits out of the people working up there.

We decided to start from Elmendorph Military Air Base across Fish Creek from Fifth Avenue. There were two houses that were shook off the bluff, and one sitting there at the bottom looking as nice as ever. From there we followed the fault all the way to a subdivision called Turnagan by the Sea. There was noticable damage along our walk, most of it minor, such as foundations and sections of a road sunk several feet. Turnagan by the Sea was a mess. Many houses and cars went down with the earth like it had marbles for support.

The earthquake wave effected many communities all the way to California. The worst damage was mostly on the Alaska Coast, places like Valdez, Seward and Kodiak and many more small villages up and down the coast. Kodiak had fishing boats gushed right into the buildings. Seward had lots of damage, wrecking fuel tanks, and other damage. Valdez was totalled. The big wave lifted a ship that was secured to the dock and then dropped it to the bottom of the ocean. It totalled the truck and killed the driver and a dog. One of the ship's crew held his camera on the rail and took pictures while all of this was going on. Valdez was located on the very end of the channel and took full force of the pressure. It wiped out the town. A safer location was chosen for building the new Valdez.

MAYOR OF DELTA JUNCTION

Appointed Mayor

How does a person become a mayor? In my case, there was no election. In Delta Junction, the city council made the choice, and that's how I became mayor. I didn't know beans about handling such a responsible job. As far as that goes, nobody else knew any more than I did.

We didn't even have money for postage or paper. We all kicked in a dollar for starters and we received an antiquated mimeograph machine from the Army or somebody. Barbra Prindle volunteered to type for us.

Mile 1422

I often wondered about the name of our city, "Delta Junction." The citizens of our town hadn't had a chance to decide what our town name should be. The Post Office at Big Delta had moved to the Delta intersection and named it Delta Junction. So, I put an article in our local weekly paper, saying "What are your feelings about the name of your city? We didn't have a chance to name it!" A different article in the paper said, "Ray wants to change the name of our city." Wow! What a mob of people turned up, almost all business people. There was much discussion. Some said they would have to buy new letterhead, that people would be confused, and why should the name be changed. I reminded them our new governor didn't change letterhead. He just crossed out the old governor's name and used his own name. Well, the town is still Delta Junction.

From way back, the area for miles around was called Big Delta. If your quarters were eight miles north of Delta junction, you would be in Big Delta. Their citizens there love that name and so do I. If anyone suggested Delta Junction should share that name I would have been dead set against it, because the name Big Delta is a solid name from way back.

I wasn't disappointed that Delta Junction didn't want to change the town name, but I thought the reasons were pretty weak. Suggestions were made like "Deltanna," where the Delta River and the Tanana River meet, or "Buffalo Center," which was named by the Bureau of Land Management very close to the Alaska Highway and the Junction.

My favorite name would have been Mile 1422. I didn't think anyone else would be interested in such a simple name, but that name would have become known worldwide. Alaska has a mile post every mile. Working for highways all those years, we all depended on the Mile Posts for our location every day. I never mentioned this choice to anyone in Delta. They would have thought I was nuts. But I thought it could have been Delta - Mile 1422.

Another good name would have been Little Delta – Mile 1422. Or just Little Delta. I was surprised that not one business enterprise in Delta Junction thought Mile 1422 was worthy to capitalize on. From working on the construction of the Alaska Highway since the time I was seventeen, in my head the idea to use Mile Posts was so strong that it never goes away.

Fixing the Furnace at 70 Below

What other responsibilities did a mayor have? The Delta citizens never heard about most of the important things that happened, such as the toilet that wasn't working. The temperature was -70 F when I got a call about midnight that the red light was on, indicating that furnace's heat dropped to a certain temperature at the Town Hall. There wasn't much I could do but put on my warmest clothes and see what was wrong. Of course the fuel barrel was empty. I had to search around for a clean barrel and the hand fuel pump. At that cold temperature you have to be careful with a fuel pump hose or it might break if you try to bend it too much. I got the fuel to the lean-to garage for our fire truck with icicles hanging on the water pump to the gravel floor. I transferred the fuel from my barrel to the furnace barrel, then got the air out of the system and it started just fine. I had to charge that fuel to one of our trucks so that everything was hunky-dory. We had orders from Fairbanks to cut our thermostat down to 65F when it got that cold. I had to tell Fairbanks that our furnace was running steady 24 hours a day trying to reach 60F. (My wife would put on her eiderdown underwear just to keep warm.)

Funding the Firefighter Pie

We tried raising money for the Fire Department. If you paid $20 a year and we made a call to your property, you didn't owe us anything. If you didn't become a member, you had to pay quite a high figure. Well, that went over like a lead balloon. How can you bill someone that has lost everything? We just let it go if they didn't have the money. Actually, we didn't ask for any money anyway.

I had a great idea on how to raise a little money for our Fire Department. All we had to do was to levy a small tax with many exceptions, which included anything grown or produced locally. Large items like a snow machine or automobiles were not taxed at all. The tax was very liberal and I thought it would pass. Some of the residents, though, were from places like New York, Los Angeles, and other large cities. They didn't trust their city fathers that the tax would only be on for a short time. Nobody would believe it. I voted against it myself the third time it came up to a vote.

My mayor's job of trying to raise money for the city was a challenge. Barbra Prindle, our city clerk, would type for us, so I thought I would make up a little book with some Alaska stories in it. The last page was a place for a certificate that said, "This certifies that (blank) has gone through the trials and tribulations to reach Mile 1422, the end of the Alaska Highway at Delta Junction on this date (blank)." It had the Delta Junction seal and was signed by myself as mayor, Barbra Prindle, City Clerk; Jon Duphendack, Delta Chamber President, and Deane Goodwin, Delta Hostess.

The best time to write stories is when the weather is extremely cold, so I went at it that winter. I had already written some stories, and I added some new ones. Barbra Prindle did the typing and we spun the books off on our "new" mimeograph.

The Chamber thought it was a great idea, so we put the little books up for sale at the information triangle for $1.00 each. It was surprising how many of these humble books we sold. Now that we were in the "bucks," our fire department could buy a piece of pie for each fireman who was at a fire with city money. I heard a little gossip through the grapevine that we were a little too extravagant with the city's money. We were going to have our pie.

I enjoyed being a mayor. I just wished I could have been a better one. It was a learning process, on the-job training.

Thanks for the Fire Truck, Betty Crocker®

A few years after I was mayor, in 1970, Mrs. Deane Goodwin found out that it would be possible to get a new fire truck with Betty Crocker coupons. This gigantic project started out with contacting people and places by mail and by mouth, spreading the word that Deane Goodwin was collecting General Mills Betty Crocker® coupons for a fire truck. Someone made contact with the Arthur Godfrey radio show and his words about our effort were heard in every state in the union. Thank-you, Arthur! Deane managed to organize a crew of women (including my Ma) to remove excess paper and bind coupons with rubber bands, 100 to the bundle. A truck from Minnesota hauled the coupons to Betty Crocker®/General Mills. The <u>Delta Midnight Sun</u> reported on July 20, 1972, that "it took 6,960,000 coupons and $5,500 in cash."

TRIPS OUTSIDE, 1970'S

The Doctor's New Truck

The times were altogether different in 1972, twenty years after our first trip in 1952. We weren't on easy street by any means, but life's trials and tribulations were easing up. Our kids were young adults and were drifting away from home one by one. We were beginning to feel a new freedom.

The trip started out as a whim. We were visiting Dr. and Mrs. Murphy one weekend when a discussion came up about the new truck he had ordered from Bowdle, South Dakota. He wondered if he should ship it up or have someone drive it up because he wasn't able to take enough time off himself to do it. A little light bulb lit up in my head and I said, "Lucy and I will drive it up for you."

I was surprised when Dr. Murphy said, "You've got yourself a deal."

Trip of '72 with VW Bug

It was early in September, crisp cool air warning us that winter was just around the corner. Lucy and I talked over how we would travel. We bought a little tent made especially to mount on top of our little Volkswagen (VW) Bug. We decided we would stay at a motel one night on our trip. The other nights would all be in our little tent. We prepared ourselves with a tie down to secure the VW to the truck bed for the return trip and with a few changes of clothes, and we were ready to go.

It was snowing when we left Delta Junction. Our little tent worked fine. It opened in 10 or 15 seconds, it took me several minutes each time to unsnap the fasteners because they would be frozen.

It snowed all the way to the Montana border. My Gosh! I had forgotten what a long trip it was to Montana. When we got close to the Montana/Canadian border, we got into a real snow storm. We could hardly read the highway signs, some not at all. Even when we stopped, they were so plastered with wet snow we couldn't read them. I said, "This is the night we're going to stay in a roadhouse."

Luckily we were able to read a sign that directed us to a Canadian Government hotel. Wow! What luxury -- a beautiful huge room including a TV and lots of hot water for a bath. I told Lucy it was too nice to sleep in, that we should stay awake all night so we didn't waste it.

Lucy said, "You can stay awake all night. I'm going to sleep."

We took hot baths in the morning too, just to get our money's worth. The morning was glorious. It had quit snowing and the sun was shining. We were in for a beautiful day. We stopped at Black Eagle, close to Great Falls to visit our friends, Basil and Gina Pizzini. Basil made a polenta and Gina hovered over us like a mother hen. That evening, Basil asked me where we were going in South Dakota. I told him we had arranged to meet my Uncle Eddie and Aunt Alice at Bowdle the next day. Basil got out the road atlas so I could show him. I was shocked to see how far we still had to go.

"My Gosh! We still have 900 miles to go. We'll have to leave real early in the morning," I told Lucy.

Gina said, "You kids aren't going any place in the morning till you have breakfast." I told Gina we were leaving about 2 a.m.

"Ray! You wouldn't do that," Gina said. She didn't believe me.

I woke up at 2 a.m. and loaded the car and talked quietly to their dog so it wouldn't bark. Then I woke Lucy. She walked to the car in a daze, plunked down in the seat and immediately fell asleep. I reluctantly left without a cup of coffee.

I drove 200 miles before I came to an all-night restaurant where I stopped and had a couple of cups of coffee and filled the thermos. I drove another hundred miles before Lucy awakened.

"How would you like some coffee?"

"That would be great!" I handed Lucy the full thermos. She had no idea we had stopped. After about 600 miles I made a wrong turn and discovered we had gone about 100 miles out of our way. The turn I had taken was going somewhat parallel, but gradually headed north. We had to drive 100 miles straight south to get to the highway we were supposed to be on. We did meet my Uncle Eddie and Aunt Alice at the little town of Bowdle and had a great visit, our first get-together in 20 years.

The Chevy dealer had Dr. Murphy's truck all ready to go. All we had to do was drive our VW up onto the truck bed. We loaded the VW, bound it down, bid farewell to my Uncle Eddie and Aunt Alice, and we were ready to roll toward home.

Chinook

We picked up 2 tons of dog feed for Dr. Murphy, covered it with visqueen (a clear plastic sheeting), and tied it down. The only other thing left to do was to shop around for a light ladder so we could get up over the high sides into the rear of the truck in order to get to our tent on top of the VW.

The snow was pretty much melted on the southern end of our trip, so road conditions looked very good. The new truck was fun to drive. Lucy kept herself busy knitting, so time went pretty fast and we enjoyed the crisp, clear weather. That lasted until we got about 100 miles south of Whitehorse.

We met a car coming our way flashing his lights. "I wonder what he's doing that for?" I said.

Soon another car flashed his lights. "Maybe the dog feed has slipped down and the visqueen is flapping," I told Lucy. I stopped on a straight stretch and checked the load. Everything looked fine.

In a few more miles we discovered what the travelers were warning us about. Suddenly, our cab windows fogged up and we were on wet ice. A Chinook! The truck swerved from side to side. I touched the brakes gently to gain control and slow down. As soon as we hit the ice, we saw a pickup that had rolled over, the camper squashed, things strewn all over. We got very cautious after that.

I cut our speed down to 15 mph and even at that I felt queasy. I drove several miles like this until we came to a hill about 500 yards long. I geared down, because I didn't dare use the brakes. It was a mistake. I was one gear too low. My wheels didn't turn; they just slid. I lost control of the truck.

A pickup had stopped at the bottom of the hill. Nonchalant, the driver got out of his pickup and just stood there. In the meantime, I was sliding down the hill crossways, first one way and then the other. Terrible visions were in my head. I could see us going over the fill, wrecking the new truck, and our sweet little Bug. This was one of the three times I've been "scared to death" in my life. I kept turning the wheel first one way then the other way, just inches from plummeting over the bank.

Lucy never uttered a sound. She just kept knitting like crazy.

When we finally got to the bottom, I tip-toed the truck to a straight stretch and shut the truck off.

"I am not moving this truck another inch till this ice melts." I was that scared.

We were parked there about an hour before it began to feel like it was warming up. A couple of trucks with chains on were going south and that started cracking the ice. I finally decided to give it a try. We drove very cautiously for a few miles and came to a hill. I pulled to the side as far as I dared and stopped. "I am going to walk this entire hill to see if it is safe," I told Lucy when she asked why I stopped. It was a mile or so to the bottom, but I checked every inch of it.

"When we get to Whitehorse, I'm going to shop for some tire chains," I told Lucy. There weren't many places open because it was the weekend, but we found one place that had a single set of chains, no duals available. They had to do. We felt a lot better having the chains, even though the crisis was over with. You never know what lies ahead.

Rescue by Candy Bar

We had enough Canadian money for a light supper plus $10 American we were saving for the American side. After supper we had just enough Canadian money left to buy a deck of cards and one candy bar. We back tracked for a campground we had noticed on our way into Whitehorse. About three miles out of town, all the truck lights went out. We were close to a little road where the ditch was fairly shallow and flat, so that's where we perched for the night.

We thought we were going to have a nice evening playing cards, but with no lights, we just sat in the dark truck and visited till we decided to try to sleep in our little tent on top of the Bug. I didn't know for sure what I would do about the situation in the morning.

I found the fuse panel and found a burned-out fuse. A new fuse wouldn't do me any good, though, even if I had had one, unless I could find out what blew it out. I've wasted a lot of time looking for a short in automotive wiring, so I didn't have much confidence. First, I checked the battery connections. They were fine. Then I looked elsewhere, and luck was with me. I found the shorted wire on the bottom of the steering column. It's a good thing I wasn't a litterbug and hadn't thrown out the wrapper of candy bar we'd enjoyed the previous night. I used the outer wrapper to insulate the wire with and made a fuse from the inner foil wrapper. Everything worked fine then and we made the last 600 miles home.

Trip of '77

A year after I retired, Lucy and I made one more trip "outside," and we decided to make a full ring around the United States. We started in Montana, east to New York, down to Florida and down the Keys. We purposely drove the old coast roads, except when we needed the rest areas along the highways. Then we followed close to Mexico over to California and then up to Washington and toward home. Lucy was always ready for a trip. She loved to go.

MY TUNDRA ROSE

Lucy's Job with the Pipeline

Times were changing for the better in the early 1970's. The Alaska Pipeline was under construction from Prudhoe to Valdez. Big Delta and Delta Junction were right in the middle of it. A main camp was located at Big Delta and several local people worked there, including my wife Lucy, my daughter Judy, and Betty Nistler. They worked twelve hour days, seven days a week.

Lucy cleaned sixty rooms a day. She lost so much weight that her shoes looked large on her feet. At that time we were paying our mortgage off as quick as we could. Lucy was making $16.00 an hour, a lot more than I was being paid by the Road Commission, and she made four mortgage payments a month while I made one. We were able to pay most of our mortgage off in one year.

My Retirement in 1977

People in Delta Junction were good to me. I had the pleasure of working my last 18 years there at Mile 1422. A great retirement party was held for me in 1977 at the old Trophy Lodge. I'll never forget it. I didn't want a party. But I had the most fun! There were people from 100 to 200 miles away who attended my celebration. The guys I worked with built me a beautiful model of my favorite truck, a big

Oshkosh with a V plow, a side delivery plow, a side wing plow, and a belly blade. This model sits on a window shelf here in Minnesota.

Sharing Her Life With Me

My Lucy got cancer. She passed away in January 1986 after sharing her life with me for 38 years. I didn't have enough available money for the funeral, because Lucy and I had been putting all our wages toward the mortgage. The new bankers who didn't know me wouldn't loan me the money. My daughter Jewel did.

Lonesome

After my wife Lucy died, I was a very lonesome person. I realized what life might have been like for my Grandpa on the farm after Grandma died and Grandpa was all alone. He must have talked to the horses, cows, pigs, and dog. I know now why he took me to the field to have me with him, even if there wasn't much for me to do after the rocks were picked and moved to the edge of the field. It was the loneliness that Grandpa tried to overcome. I'm sure the animals looked Grandpa in the eye when he made his rounds in the morning and night. I think the hardest part for Grandpa was going back into the house, poking the fire in the stove and frying a couple of eggs and looking across the table where Grandma would have been sitting in her favorite chair. I can't help thinking how different life was on the farm when he was alone.

Tundra Rose

I fell in love
> *with a Tundra Rose*
Thirty
> *and eight years ago*

She was beautiful
> *fresh*
as a dew drop
> *in early morn*
For this Tundra Rose
> *I was born*

She reared our five
> *introduced them to God*
Kept them so very clean
> *my Tundra Rose*
> *from Alaska's sod*

When summer ends
> *petals wilt and fall*
My precious Tundra Rose
> *you are still as beautiful*
> *as I recall*
It breaks my heart
> *to see the Pain*
> *tears falling*
For my Tundra Rose
> *like rain*

Dear God,
> *bring the wilted petals back*

And sparkle from the dew
> *we give you the praise and glory*

Because our love is True

I'm asking you again, dear Lord,
> *for a few more precious years*

To be with my darling Tundra Rose
> *end my weeping tears.*

The Great Potlatch

I entered the house
> *feeling a little reluctant.*

Would I feel relief,
> *could I control my grief?*

They were all there, the house was overflowing
> *with people and their love.*

A special message
> *from God above.*

This is the fourth day,
> *much food has been prepared and consumed.*

Many kind words were spoken, warm hugs,
> *hands shaken.*

Friends and relatives have come from far and wide.
      Northway, California, Anchorage, Delta, Tanana, and Dot Lake,
To give our family support and love.
      To help ease the pain and help ease the heartache.

I don't think any Great Chief has been shown greater tribute
      than Lucy's family is bestowing on her this day.
Love was static, love was in their eyes,
      love was in their hearts, they felt the loss deeply, too.

I felt reluctant no more.
I feel the true meaning and purpose of a potlatch.
Thank God their heritage has survived.

Lucy's Pa, ninety years old, unable to see, unable to hear,
      Sitting alone, not in charge within himself,
Although still in charge through the family blood.
Thank God, the younger generation
      is carrying on their tradition.
I'm proud my children have Eskimo blood.

WHEN YOU ARE NOT THE SON BUT HAVE YOUR OWN

The Scare of My Life

It was a typical weekend. We planned to go moose hunting. We wouldn't have starved without a moose, but we couldn't afford fresh milk even though there were two dairy farms close to Fairbanks. Fresh fruit was a luxury, watermelons were $1.00 a pound, oranges were 35 cents. Fresh meat was out of the question. My kids were raised on canned or powdered milk. We didn't suffer.

My dad, my wife Lucy, myself, and our 5 year old son Jerry, were ready to leave for the woods. Our daughter Judy was about four years old. She wanted to go too because Jerry was going. I told Judy, "We have to be quiet or the moose will run away. You are a blabber jack."

We had to leave Judy home with our niece for the week we were gone. The weather was bad and we never saw a moose. When we came back, we took our belongings out of my dad's car because my mother and dad were going hunting for a few more days. My dad had just driven away, heading the same place where we were hunting before, when our neighbor lady dashed over to our house.

"Was that your little girl riding on the rear bumper?"

"Oh, my God! It must be Judy."

I hopped into my car and took off like a rocket. I drove about three miles and didn't catch up with my parents. I turned around like a maniac and I met my dad's car. I honked my horn and flashed my lights but my dad and mother couldn't expect me to be going in that direction. I had to go past them again and saw Judy hanging on the rear door latch with her feet on the bumper. I tooted my horn and flashed my lights but my dad wouldn't stop. He must have thought I was some crazy person playing games. The only thing I could do was to pass my Dad again. The road was clear so with my lights flashing and horn blaring I stomped on the accelerator and passed my dad again. I must have been going 80 or 90 miles an hour. I whipped around again with a big cloud of dust and drove right toward his car so he couldn't get around me.

Pa said, "How did you get here?" I ran behind my Pa's car and grabbed Judy and squeezed her till it hurt. (I was telling this story to a friend and I said, "I don't think I spanked her." Judy said, "Yes you did, Daddy." Honey, if I did, I didn't spank you very hard.)

What made the big mix up was the new bridge had just opened for traffic the day before and my folks didn't know it. That's why they couldn't figure how I could be ahead of them. I had crossed the new bridge and they took the long way. I still shudder while writing this story, thinking of what could have happened. (Honey, I squeezed you hard but I spanked you gently, honest.)

Jerry's Life Race

Lucy drove Jerry to Anchorage, Alaska from our home in Fairbanks to participate in a 26 mile race. After the race, Jerry decided he wanted to join the Navy instead of going home with his mother.

Jerry went through boot camp and did OK, but when he went to a trade school, he became schizophrenic also, as happened to my brother Bruce. He has gone through many difficult times, the same as my brother Bruce did. Jerry cannot survive without his medicine.

One time he ran away from the hospital and hitch-hiked 25 miles on the freeway in his hospital slippers and his nightgown.

Jerry was married for 10 years, but it was difficult. It is still difficult for him to live on his own. He stays in a care home where they are good to him, and the Navy hospital treats him well.

First Hunt

Tamarack glistens with a golden glow.
      Birch trees are turning yellow-and refuse to grow.
A frosty chill is in the air.
      Dear God, do you have a moose to spare?

Meat's been on the table—along with grace.
      Hotdogs and beans have taken their place.
So, up in the hills we must proceed
      To hunt and fish so we may eat.

Wake up, son, the sky is bright,
      Thank God for the rest we got last night.
A big breakfast is in the making
      Biscuits and eggs and crispy bacon.

"Let's go, Pa, let's get a moose
      Before he runs away."
"Hold it, son, let's figure this out.
      Where can he go this day?"

John made his stalk in true scout fashion
      as perfect as could be.
I held my breath to hear that shot

(my boy would make the kill)
But nothing broke the silence,
  except my pounding heart.
"What gives here, son, why don't you shoot?
  This is no way to start."

"I'm sorry, Pa," is all that he could say,
  "I'm sorry, Pa," he said.
"When I got close and saw his eyes
  and his enormous head
His kingly crown, his snuggly nose,
  I think, Dad, you know the rest."

It's much later in the season now.
  The bull has lost his senses.
His smarts are gone when nature calls
  And all he thinks—is cows.

"Now listen, son, you sit right here.
  I'm going to give a call
To that bully moose
  that you let go this fall."

The mountain shook when I heaved my chest
  and gave the final blast.
He heard my call and came sliding down
  the mountain with a crash.

Here he was so close—I could see
  his eyelash and a mole.

My time had come to show my son
       A task—a task that must be done.

I've shot a moose a dozen times
       and no thrill it was to me.
For food it was to raise these kids
       and get them off my knee.

I had to study this fellow
       A lot longer than I should.
John said, "Dad, what are you waiting for?
       You rather that I could?"

Seems like I'm getting sentimental
       as the years go rolling by
But thinking of our long winter I'd better go ahead
       and shoot this moose—and do it quick
       so he will surely die.

I had to pull the trigger.
       There was no out for me.
He buckled up—and fell to earth
       This kingly beast—how sad.

The big thing I tell my boy
       is not to pull the trigger
But what must be done for half a ton
       or maybe even bigger.

Now this here story is for sons to read

---

and to THINK what lies ahead.
The day will come when you're not the son
    but will have your own instead.

-- Dedicated to my youngest son, John who was found frozen to death in 1982 at the age of 29.

This is one of the last things that Ray's son, John, wrote while in his little cabin which was only five rounds high, located on top of a hill overlooking the Alaska range.

I'm Going Home, I'm Going Home

By John R.

I'm going home, I'm going home,
    sometimes ashes, sometimes dust,
Sometimes chocolate, sometimes rust.

Newness, oldness, all the same,
    knowing things just never change,
Taking time to realize things are as they are,
    because what has happened is good by far.

Meeting new ones, seeing old ones,
    giving oration of your life.
This is the gold of your strife,
    it keeps the fire burning.
It makes the day go by,
    it makes the value of living,
Not just time passing, why?

To be accepted as you were
          so many years ago,
And not as a perfect stranger
          whose values must be shown.
The things now
          I think I've found,
          really do spring up from the ground.

They make the world on a level keel,
          not much credence to concrete and steel.
They say,
          if you have to stay,
          then go ahead,
Come and see me, the door's always open in your stead.
          Any time, any place, is not like being there
          for all to grace.

A Letter to my youngest son John, who was found frozen to death in 1982, age of 29.

Dear John,

I've wanted to write to you ever since you left us on December 19, 1982. I mentioned this to your Mom shortly after you were gone, but she became hysterical, thinking that I was out of my mind. I wasn't, John, in fact, many things were becoming clearer.

Your Mom is gone now, too. She got cancer in October of 1985 and passed away several months later. I've had a lot of time to think since then.

After your body was found frozen about a mile from your cabin, and we buried you, I had many sleepless nights, especially the first six months. You were on my mind twenty-four hours a day. I tried to think of other things, but I couldn't do it. I'd lay down, and my thoughts would be about you. I'd jump up out of bed and almost physically shake away a fit of depression.

Your Mom and I knew you had a problem with alcohol, although we didn't want to admit that you were alcoholic. We had never seen you drunk. You always spared us the embarrassment of coming home in that condition.

When we visited you in Charleston, SC, and you said I'd have to drive because you didn't have a driver's license, I think we knew then. We were reminded again when Mrs. Brown, the nice old lady you stayed with in Anchorage, asked us to talk to you about drinking. I said to your Mom, "John is a grown boy. What can we say?"

Looking back on the day of the funeral, it was the coldest day of the winter, 55 degrees below zero. My pickup froze on the way to the church because I'd neglected to check the anti-freeze, and it was weak.

Your Grandpa and Grandma didn't make it to the funeral. The temperature had dropped to 60 degrees below zero at Delta Junction that morning. I didn't expect them to drive one-hundred miles in that cold weather for the funeral, but I was hoping that they would make it in the spring when we buried you. They still don't know where you are buried, or for that matter, where your Mom is buried either.

We met you in the spring at Wasila, after your winter in Big Lake. We should have recognized then that there were changes in your personality. You were so unkempt, your clothes shabby, your hair long and shaggy.

That reminds me of the long hair incident that happened before you went in the Submarine service for the U.S. Navy. I remember fussing about giving you a trim. You were slow to respond because it seemed to be how the typical American boy was wearing his hair. I didn't really mind, clean, well-groomed, long hair, at least reasonably long. It did bug me because it seemed more like a cause against the establishment and house rules. I remember throwing the clippers on the floor and breaking them. John, this bothered me for a long time after you left home. I should have had more control.

That's the reason I wanted to give you something special when you left home for the Navy. I didn't know what to give you, but it had to be something that I valued and cared for. I thought of the little stone our friend, Mr. Levit from Borrow gave me. The little stone was shaped like a perfect little mukluk, even the ookrook bottom had worn through. The stone didn't have five cents in monetary value, but it was very precious to me. I often thought of it and wondered if you still had it, or if it meant anything to you. I looked for it in your personal things after you left us, John, but I didn't find it.

The haircutting incident bothered me for a long time after you left for the Navy. That's why I mentioned it when we visited you at Charleston. We were spending a beautiful day at the beach. We were about the only people there. The local people didn't spend much time there in the winter, only an occasional jogger or someone walking their dog.

I remember that you jogged too. You were so durable. A couple miles up and down the beach, and you didn't even breathe hard. Your mom and I admired you.

We were having such a wonderful visit that I didn't want to spoil it with a man-to-man talk, but it still bothered me about that haircut. When I mentioned the incident, you said, "I don't remember that, Dad." God bless you, Son.

I wanted to talk to you man-to-man when we were prospecting. You'd think in six weeks that we spent at our rough camp, there would have been a time when I could have told you some of my trials and tribulations, but I didn't want to spoil it with that kind of talk.

I still remember our visit on the beach. I brought up some things about how you were doing things. You told me, without malice, and in such a way not to hurt my feelings, that it really wasn't any of my business. After a few seconds pause, I thought about it, and I said, "You're right, John. You're a grown man, and you don't have to account to me about your life."

I remember when you were staying with us, helping us get our new house started. We were living in the cache. Your mom and I slept in our little tent on top of the sawhorses. The tent kept the mosquitoes at bay. You only had enough room to lay your sleeping bag on the floor. Remember how your muscles tightened up on your back from peeling logs?

When you walked to the Bulls-Eye about a mile from our house, your mom and I wondered if you went to drink, but we didn't say a word to you. We were relieved when you returned home in less than an hour. We didn't ask, and we couldn't tell if you had anything to drink.

Sometime later, you mentioned that you met a wonderful girl named Connie. We thought you met her in Delta. When you told us you met her at the Bulls-Eye, I remember teasing you that I thought you found a beautiful young virgin in the bushes close to your cabin. John, I'm sorry that I didn't know you were so lonely for female companionship. I should have known because I would have been very lonely too.

When we cleared out your cabin at Delta, we found a couple of letters that you had written to Connie, and also a letter you had written to me, asking for help, as well as a letter to Mom that you hadn't finished.

John, I never realized until you were gone how much you and I were alike. We didn't want you to go to Delta in November to start building a cabin. I worried your tent would catch on fire. Your mom and I mentioned what an easy winter it would be if you stayed with us. We wouldn't be pressed to do much because winter would put everything on hold until spring. We could visit, play pinochle, snowshoe or ski, and just enjoy life. You insisted that you wanted to go. I would have gone too, John. I was just like you.

Your mom didn't want to save anything from your cabin. We threw most of your clothes in the deep pit you worked so hard to dig for your toilet pit.

We looked carefully through all your papers. We saw that you wrote your thoughts down just like I'm doing now. I was surprised to see your poem, and I liked it. I included it in my collection of poems.

John, I feel better writing to you. My book is dedicated to my Pa, and your Grandpa, but it's also the story that I wanted to tell you, and it never seemed to be the right time. I don't know why, John, unless it's because we were so much alike. Like the letter you wrote to me—and never mailed.

Your mom and I loved you very much. Rest in peace, John.

Love,
Dad

Our Visit

"Why do you squeeze me so hard, Dad?"
I want to tell you I love you, son.
You look so strong and handsome,
your clean white shirt
in contrast with your black hair and dark features.
I remember it well.

It's been awhile, John, since we've visited,
although a day hasn't gone by without a thought of you in my head.
I think of so many things we did together.
Our winter and summer campouts with Troop 76.

You and your fellow scouts cheered like crazy,
when you awoke and came to the big camp fire
and found out it was 42 below zero.
You earned your 100 Degree Below patch.
It was a challenge – but you did it.

I remember when you learned to swim at summer camp.
You wanted to swim that mile over and over.
After the sixth time the counselors said
Enough was enough.
I swam one mile with you, John. Do you remember?

When you went into the Navy right out of high school,
the submarine was your choice.
I didn't like it.
Memories came to me. Our escort sunk a sub off the coast of New
Caledonia.
I heard some cheers.

I saw one sub come into Pearl Harbor with its periscope bent over 90
degrees.
It's dangerous, John. I didn't like it.
If my dad said, "Don't do it," I'd have done it anyway.
I understand, John.

I remember so well.

You were proud of your submarine.

I would have been too.

Your invitation for Christmas dinner aboard your ship was so special.

The only place we couldn't visit was where you worked, the nuclear section.

You were our qualified "nuke man."

I'm sorry, John.

I can't write anymore this morning. My dream was so real

I could feel my muscles still flexing from squeezing you

when I woke up.

Bless you, John. I love you so much.

ROMANCING AT MY AGE

Looking for Company

After Lucy died, I would visit my family as often as I could without being a nuisance. I would go to Alaska Land, a park in Fairbanks where the tourists could park their trailer for a few days, and strike up a conversation and ask them how they enjoyed Alaska, etc. Most of them were willing to talk and the general opinion was they were having a good time.

Things went fairly well till winter came along. Before my wife died, we did everything together and a big share of my life was to make things more comfortable for both of us, but now my life was in limbo. I had lots of things I could do, but my heart wasn't in it.

I received a letter notifying me there would be a high school class reunion in June in Minnesota. All these years in Alaska, I never could afford to go to these affairs. But just maybe . . . I would be lucky enough to meet somebody that would look at this old geezer. I started to make plans and save some money. I called my Uncle Robert and Aunt Darlene in St Paul to see if I could stay with them for a few days. They said, "Come on down."

Looking for a Wife

This was a whole school reunion, so there was a mob of people. The first day, I only saw 2 or 3 people I knew, but I was told that our class of '43 would have our own picnic the next day. I looked the ladies over to see who was hanging around the bar (I was fussy). Then I spotted Patricia Bergh stretched out on a park bench. I went over there and struck up a conversation and had a feeling I could get along with this lady. Before the party broke up, I asked her if she cared to correspond with me.

She said, with a tone like *Ho Hum*, "I guess it would be all right."

I wrote to her every night for six months and she answered me about 3/4ths of the time. I must have been a pest. I waited till her grandson was born, and then I flew to Minnesota to get acquainted better with Pat.

Dear Pat,

I'm all alone in my cabin,
> *These long winter nights,*
Living on dreams
> *Of you making me happy*
And me reviving a happiness
> *That you once knew.*
Letters are nice,
> *And serve a purpose,*
But lack that tender touch.
> *The sparkle of a lover's eye,*
> *A real whisper in my ear,*
From a sensuous voice that says,
> *I love you dear.*

This verse is more than just
     A passing fantasy
It's from a lonely heart
     To a lonely heart.
Looking for a purpose
     A bond
     A buddie
     A sweetheart
Someone to share the best of the rest
     Of our lives.
To make a house – a home.

Love, Ravin

[Valentine's Day 1988, illustrated with sparkly heart stickers]

After meeting all her family and attending her church, I decided I'd better go back to Fairbanks. As soon as I arrived, I called my daughter June.

The first thing she said to me was, "Dad, you better go sign up for the $1,000 dividend check. This is the last day."

I said, "Honey, I've been gone over ninety days. I won't qualify."

June said, "Try it anyways. You might get it." So I went to the dividend office and told the lady I would like to sign up for the dividend check.

A dour lady gave me a form that asked why I was gone over 90 days: in the hospital, attending school, in jail, etc. I wrote, "I'm looking for a wife." When she took my form, I observed her. When she got to "wife," she smiled a big smile and said, "You might get it."

And I did. Oh! Great Alaska. The next year, I tried it again, but there was a handwritten note: "You better look for a wife in Alaska."

1988 Courting Pat

Romancing in your sixties is quite different from romancing in your teens, when you were daring and reckless. *What will my kids think? What will Patti's family say?* I need not have worried. Both sides were happy for us.

When you haven't seen someone for 40 years, you expect some surprises. After I was in Pat's home for a few days, I went down to the basement for something. *Uh-oh! What am I getting into?* I saw six or seven 5 gallon jugs of wine. I didn't say anything to Pat. Time would tell. I would learn Pat drank very little of anything except water, tea, coffee and milk or a social glass of wine once in a Blue Moon. Pat made these wines from wild grapes, dandelions or any wild berries. She couldn't stand to see them go to waste. Pat's sons "borrowed" most of it the past 18 years and I think there is still some cached in her basement.

Things started to unravel, not fall apart, but to unravel new discoveries. Pat's Border collie Sky didn't like me the minute I stepped into Pat's car. She exposed her teeth, saying to me, "This is MY car." It took six months for Sky to unravel and accept me. Then, if she had to go out, which was very seldom, she would come to my side of the bed and whisper in my ear, just as gentle as could be, "mm-mm-mm." I knew I was family.

There certainly would be some adjustments to make for both of us, although many things were in our favor. For instance, we were both raised during the Depression. But Patti had one advantage over me – she is also Scottish.

After we got reacquainted, I discovered that Patti is a nature person. For example, I tried to be helpful and clean up the yard. I trimmed a couple of trees and burnt some dead limbs. I said to Patti, "I might just as well burn this brush pile."

Patti said, "No! That's a safety refuge for the rabbits."

"Ja, sure, Patti – less work for me."

One day I said to Patti, "You should have your driveway paved so we don't drag so much mud in the house."

Patti said, "No! The paving costs too much. Take your shoes off."

I said, "I do."

After a lot of thinking on my part, I said, "Patti, I'll pay for half."

"OK," she said.

I said to Patti, "Let's try camping together."

Patti said, "Let's call it 'hitched.' I don't like your Alaska term – it sounds too temporary."

The first summer I brought Pat to Alaska, I drove all over to get her acquainted with my country. We wound up at Circle, a small village of half a dozen cabins, right on the shores of the mighty Yukon River.

"If you want to become an Alaskan there are things you have to do. Number one is to pee in the Yukon."

"Where should I go?" she asked.

"Anywhere. There's not a soul to watch you."

So she did. Now I knew I had the right partner.

Patti doesn't make any bones about us not being married – only hitched. We were coming "outside" to Minnesota one fall when we decided to try a new route to cross the Canadian border. While looking at the map, I noticed a town called Oaks in North Dakota. I told Patti, "My cousin Carol lives there. I haven't seen her since she was two years old. Let's give her a call to see if she is home." We called Carol and she was thrilled to have us visit.

When we arrived she was puttering around the kitchen preparing lunch and she told us her husband would be home soon. After he arrived and introductions were made, he put his hands on his hips and said, "OK. What's the score here? Are you two married or not?"

Patti didn't hesitate a second. She said, "Save the sheets. We sleep together." I was so proud of her.

Pat and I usually went places together but one day Pat went by herself. I was sitting in the dining room drinking a cup of coffee and looking out the window and noticed a man parked his pickup and run into the woods across the road. I remembered someone had stolen a large new television from our building. Maybe this guy had a cache of stolen goods. I decided to go and investigate. By the time I got my shoes on, my coat and hat, and walked down the hall, maybe I'd be late, but I thought I'd walk down there anyway. Nothing looked suspicious, so I started back home on the other side of the road.

On my side of the road, I noticed a nice looking pair of petite white shoes partially exposed in the melting snow. I picked them up and examined them. What should I do with them? Suddenly the devil whacked his tail to get my attention and suggested I should place the shoes by the outside of my door. I responded to the devil, "Oh! That's a grand idea."

I was sitting in my favorite chair reading the paper when I heard the door latch open. Then it was silent for a few seconds. Pat stepped in.

"Whose shoes are they?"

"What shoes?"

"The ones by the door."

"Oh! Those white shoes. I found them on the side of the road," and I kept reading my paper.

Pat went into our bedroom. *She must be looking under our bed.* Pat finally came out of the bedroom with her hands on her hips and said, "OK. Where is she?"

I said, "Oh! Honey! You're jealous. Now I know you still love me. You're not a very good detective. Those shoes have laces tied together and there are a few little stones inside the shoes from the melted snow. And I love you as much as I ever did. You know I'd never bring a woman in our house and hide her under our bed."

Will You Marry Me?

I might just as well tell you how we got married. On our first trip together in Fairbanks, I thought it was time to buy a wedding ring. I wanted a genuine Alaskan wedding ring with little gold nuggets all around it, and I wanted the small diamond from my first wife's ring that gave it a sparkle and a memory of Lucy. An old friend had a jewelry store in Fairbanks and he was selling out the store because his wife died. I explained to him what I wanted. He only had one nugget ring left, so he showed it to us, and we both liked it. Pat tried it on and it was a little too large, so Mr. Larson had his craftsman measure Pat's finger and make it smaller. It fit perfectly.

Pat asked me if she could wear it. I said, "No, not till we're married."

Pat said, "I don't trust our government. If we get married they will take my small veteran's pension away and if you should die, I don't trust them to give it back to me."

Well, I carried that ring in my traveling bag twelve years. We were again in Fairbanks. We went to visit Lucy's 160 acre Native Land allotment. It is in such a beautiful setting on glacier moraine with a small lake and several ponds. Face west towards the Alaska Mountain Range, north toward Donnelly Dome or south east to the Granite Mountain Range.

The sun was shining that day and a gentle breeze fluffed Patti's hair. She sat on this huge solitary rock. I was picking blueberries on the edge of this little lake. Patti looked so beautiful with wild nature in all directions around her, and I was moved. I had her ring in my pocket. I approached the big rock. I kneeled down in the moss.

"Patti, I have something I'd like to talk to you about."

"OK. What is it?"

"Will you marry me?"

Patti hesitated, hemmed and hawed a little, and finally said, "I won't marry you, but I would like the ring."

So I said, "Oh, what the heck," and I gave her the ring. In a true sense, we have been tested by God and this rock to the end of our days and they were our witnesses.

Patti, oh! Patti, I ben tink you're grand.
Patti, oh! Patti, the best in the land.
If I should ask you
Do you love me true?
Say, "Ja, sure, you betcha.
I ben tink I do.
I do, yes, I do
Ja, sure. You betcha, I do"
If I should ask, "Do you love me true?
Say, "Ja, sure, you betcha. I ben tink I do."

Pat, My Love

One can be a friend
        And not a lover
One can be a lover
        But not a friend
That's what makes you
        So very dear to me
You're not only my lover
        But my best friend
        My wife
        My partner
        My life!

Without You
        Nothing would be the same
Without you
        Life would be very vain

For you see Pat
        You're everything
        You're my life
        You're my happiness
        You're my One & Only
I Love You So!!

Love Sweets

June 1992

EPILOGUE

Freedom

I became acquainted with a real live spider and his web when I was sitting on our open porch enjoying a cup of coffee in a gentle breeze on a June day in 2007. I discovered this small spider, about 1/3 the size of a mosquito, constructing a web. Its web material was so fine it was invisible. He dropped straight down about 14 inches and then climbed up half way very fast and changed his direction by 90 degrees. I couldn't see how he managed to run in that direction, but I couldn't see the web a dozen inches from my face.

I wondered if this interesting phenomenon had any connection with the book I've written. Does the spider and his web carry a message for me? Are the invisible strands releasing me from the bondage of knowing that my mother disowned me in her will? Is this more powerful than that albatross around my neck?

To play it safe, I accept the voodoo magic of the spider's web to release me from the albatross. Thank God! I'll be free again.

My Epitaph

Ray bought his tombstone in 2006 from Braham, Minnesota, near where his dad's farm was foreclosed on in 1929.

Raynold I. Savela

March 6, 1925 - Whenever

Thank you

Eskimo and Indian

For sharing your land with me

Alaska—God's Gifts by Ray Savela

Who owns the land we trod,
The sand—the rocks—the sod,
The birds above—the moose on earth,
And fishes of the sea?

These things aren't here to buy,
God has his ways, we have to try.
Work and sweat is the price we pay,
Then God's gifts will reach us day by day.

This land is mine as far as I can see,
To dig for gold, to chop a tree.
Flowing rivers, earth's blood line,
Ours to use—yours and mine.

The fish will die, so take a few,
And so with moose and caribou.
The tree has fallen, how fine it burns,
Wild berries will fill our urns.

Indian and Eskimo have been living here,
Long before the first reindeer.
No one make claim to God's green earth.
It was only borrowed for its worth.

White man has his ways, his school.
So many have come to seek and rule.
Title must be had, this is odd,
To land that really belongs to God.

This land is mine while I am here,
Every creek and rock and grassy spear.
When I grow old and trod no more,
This all goes back to even the score.